Cambridge IGCSE®

Computer Science

Revision Guide

David Watson and Helen Williams

CAMBRIDGE
UNIVERSITY PRESS

CAMBRIDGE
UNIVERSITY PRESS

University Printing House, Cambridge CB2 8BS, United Kingdom

Cambridge University Press is part of the University of Cambridge.

It furthers the University's mission by disseminating knowledge in the pursuit of education, learning and research at the highest international levels of excellence.

www.cambridge.org
Information on this title: education.cambridge.org

First published 2015

Printed in Poland by Opolgraf

A catalogue record for this publication is available from the British Library

ISBN 978-1-107-69634-1 Paperback

Contents

Introduction

This book has been written as a form of revision for students sitting for the IGCSE or O Level Computer Science qualification. It has been assumed throughout that the student/reader has already studied the topics to the required level and will use this book as a form of examination preparation, although it should be pointed out that this revision book is also a stand-alone source of information.

To get a good understanding of Computer Science, a student should not just rely on one source of information; it should be a combination of two or more of the following.

- Textbooks
- Notes from teachers/lesson notes
- Student's own research from libraries/Internet sites
- Revision of past papers and mark schemes
- Student's own experiences
- Revision notes based on all of the above
- A revision textbook.

This revision book closely follows the Cambridge Computer Science syllabus and covers all of the topics therein. It also takes the subject slightly further to take into account potential syllabus revisions within the near future.

There are a number of revision questions at the end of each chapter which test the understanding of the student/reader. At the very end of the book, you will find two practice papers which will cover most of the topics in the 12 chapters of this book. The two question papers closely follow the new Computer Science syllabus where papers will be sat for the first time in 2015. Sample answers have also been supplied so that the student/reader can self-assess his/her performance accordingly. The sample answers have been written by the authors. Cambridge International Examinations bears no responsibility for these answers or for the comments offered.

Computer Science is an ever-changing subject and no single textbook could hope to cover all aspects of any given topic. The student/reader needs to keep up to date with developments and keep a note of these changes to see how they impact on the subject matter of this textbook.

Different types of question

A review of Computer Science and Computer Studies past papers over the last 20 years reveals a number of different question types.

The following is a list of the most common types of question you may possibly encounter.

Name

In these questions, one word answers would suffice.

For example, '*Name three devices used to input data into a computer.*'

Acceptable answers would be: *(1) Keyboard (2) Barcode reader (3) Microphone*

Describe

In these questions, you are expected to write a sentence to describe the computing term, feature, process, etc.

For example, '*Describe what is meant by the term interrupt.*'

Acceptable answer would be: *This is a signal from a device, such as a printer, sent to the CPU; the CPU will then temporarily stop what it is doing.*

Advantages and disadvantages

In these questions, you need to write a sentence or more to describe the advantages (benefits) and disadvantages (drawbacks) of some computer process. Usually, the question may involve some comparison with another computer process.

For example, '*Give one advantage and one disadvantage of using emails rather than the normal post to send a message.*'

Acceptable answer could include: *Advantage: emails are delivered almost immediately; Disadvantage: emails require investment in a computer system.*

Trace tables

In these type of questions, you are likely to be given a flowchart and asked to trace through the flowchart using some given data. You would be expected to show the value of the variables in the table at all stages of the process.

It is a good practice to draw a line across the table after any output; this makes it easier to go back and rectify any mistake you may make. There are several examples of this type of question in chapter 6, but basically they will look like this.

x	y	z	TOTAL	OUTPUT
1	3	9	1	2
2	7	14	2	
3	1	1		
4	6	36		
5				
1	5	25	1	
2	11	132		
etc.	etc.	etc.	etc.	etc.

Flowcharts

In these questions, you would be given a computer process, such as '*using barcodes to carry out automatic stock control*'. The flowchart may have all the outline boxes but the actual items shown in these boxes might have been omitted. The items could be given in a numbered list and your task would be to place each stage in the appropriate box. You are well advised just to use the number of the item rather than trying to write the whole description in the given box.

Also remember the function of each flowchart box.

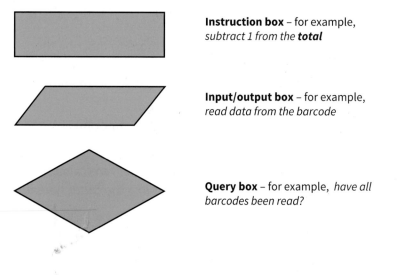

Instruction box – for example, *subtract 1 from the **total***

Input/output box – for example, *read data from the barcode*

Query box – for example, *have all barcodes been read?*

The following example illustrates this process.

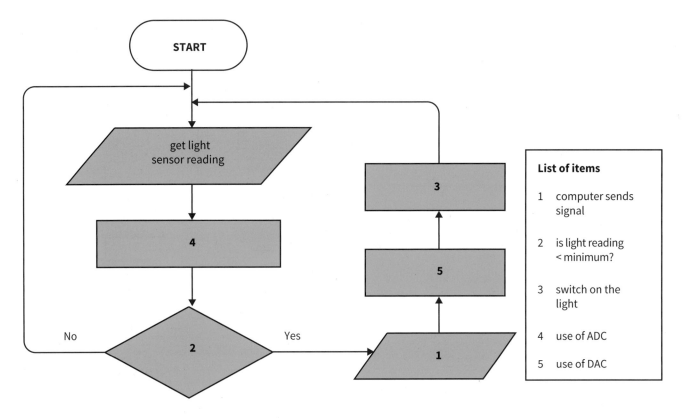

Write an algorithm

In these questions, you are likely to be given a problem which needs to be solved using either a flowchart or pseudocode (whichever is easier).

For example, *'Write an algorithm, using pseudocode or a flowchart, which inputs 100 numbers and outputs the average.'*

This can be done by pseudocode or by flowchart.

By pseudocode

total ← 0

for count ← 1 **to** 100

   input number

   total ← total + number

next count

average ← total/100

print average

By flowchart

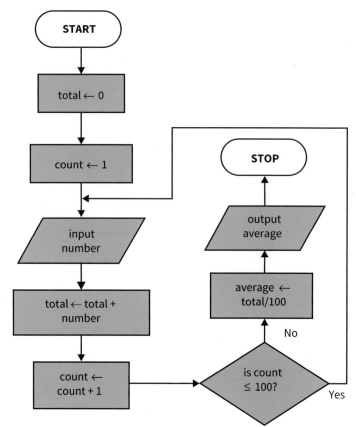

Linking boxes

In these questions, you would be given a description on one side and a computer term or application on the other side of the diagram.

You may be asked to draw arrows to show which description and computer term/application match. For example,

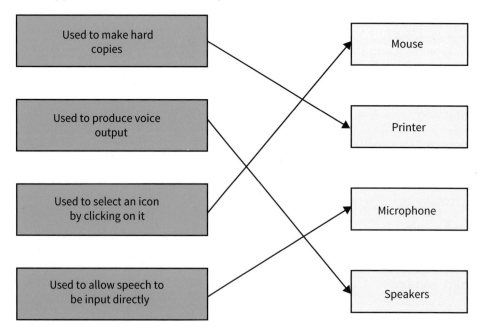

Truth tables

In these questions, you could be expected to complete a truth table to show the output from a logic gate (such as AND, OR, NOT, NAND, NOR or XOR) or from a logic network (which is a combination of these logic gates).

You may be given the binary inputs and it would only be necessary to complete the output part. For example,

A	B	C	OUTPUT X
0	0	0	1
0	0	1	1
0	1	0	1
0	1	1	0
1	0	0	0
1	0	1	0
1	1	0	0
1	1	1	0

When calculating the output for a logic network, use a pencil to show the output after each logic gate – you are less likely to make a mistake if you do this. For more examples, see chapter 9.

Drawing of logic networks

As with above, these are a recent addition to the type of questions which may be asked. You may be asked to draw a logic network based on either a given problem or a logic statement. A blank space would be provided to allow you to draw your logic network (again there are many examples of this type of question in chapter 9).

Example 1: *'Draw the logic network for X = 1 if (A = 1 OR B = 1) AND (B = NOT 1 OR C = 1)'*

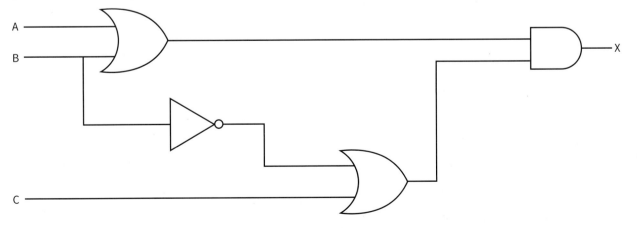

Example 2: 'Draw the logic network for the following problem.'

An alarm sounds (X =1) if certain conditions occur. These are summarised as following.

Input	Binary value	Description
H	1	height >= 0 metres
	0	height < 0 metres
S	1	speed <= 100 km/hour
	0	speed > 100 km/hour
L	1	landing gear OK
	0	landing gear failed

X = if

   landing gear OK and height < 0 metres OR

   height >= 0 metres and speed > 100 km/hour

Possible solution:

Logic statement: X = 1 if [L = 1 AND H = NOT 1] OR

                     [S = NOT 1 AND H = 1]

Giving the following logic network:

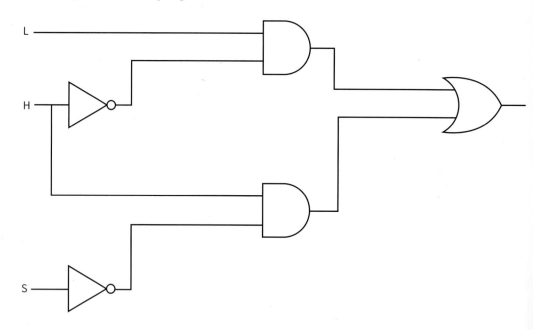

Miscellaneous types

There are many *one-off* question types set each year in Computer Science exams. Guidelines would always be given on how to set out your answers. The most common type seems to involve binary or hexadecimal registers in control applications such as elevators (lifts), robots, vending machines.

For example, the value 200 (base 10) would convert into binary as follows:

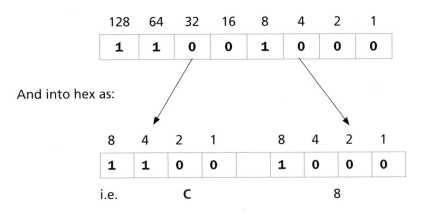

And into hex as:

i.e. C 8

Many more examples of the above question types can be found throughout the end of chapter exercises and in the two sample papers at the end of the book. When answering these questions, it is advisable to constantly refer back to this section to ensure you are correctly interpreting what is required.

1 Introduction to Computer Science

Learning Summary

In this chapter you will learn about:
- *An overview of chapters 2 to 12*
- *Components of a typical computer system*

1.1 An overview of chapters 2 to 12

Computer systems are now a very common part of our everyday lives. Nearly every application used at school/college or at work involves a computer system to some extent. Historically, not everybody has been an advocate of computer advancement. Look at the following three famous quotes and decide whether any of them have true merit.

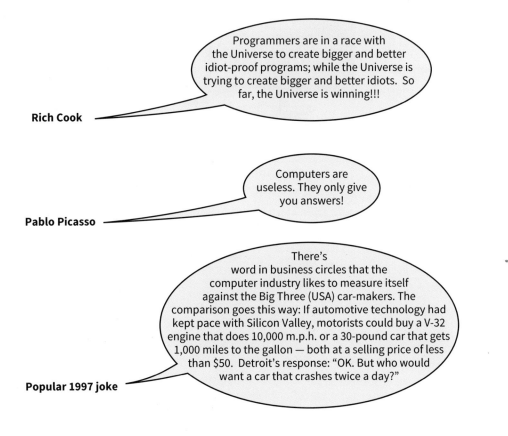

Rich Cook — Programmers are in a race with the Universe to create bigger and better idiot-proof programs; while the Universe is trying to create bigger and better idiots. So far, the Universe is winning!!!

Pablo Picasso — Computers are useless. They only give you answers!

Popular 1997 joke — There's word in business circles that the computer industry likes to measure itself against the Big Three (USA) car-makers. The comparison goes this way: If automotive technology had kept pace with Silicon Valley, motorists could buy a V-32 engine that does 10,000 m.p.h. or a 30-pound car that gets 1,000 miles to the gallon — both at a selling price of less than $50. Detroit's response: "OK. But who would want a car that crashes twice a day?"

Whatever any of us may think, computers are here to stay. We have come a long way since the Manchester 'baby' computer of 1948 – this machine could make about 700 instructions per second and used about 3.5 kilowatt of power. Sixty years later, a typical embedded computer can make 200 million instructions per second and uses only 20 milliwatts of power. The computer in 1948 nearly filled a room, whereas now a computer occupies only about 0.5 m² – a considerable size reduction! These advancements continue at an amazing rate and will be further discussed in chapter 12 as part of the future predictions.

Chapters 2 to 12 of this book will take the reader through a number of applications, discuss the impact of the Internet, look at problem-solving tools, give an insight into hardware and software currently available and how computer systems operate. The final chapter will discuss some of the possible advancements we all might see in the coming decades.

1.2 Components of a typical computer system

A typical modern computer system is a combination of hardware and software.

monitor

processor + internal memory

mouse

keyboard

Computer system

Printer

The function of the above components will be discussed in greater depth in the following chapters.

The hardware usually comprises the following.

– Input devices (such as keyboard, mouse, microphone)
– Output devices (such as monitor, printer, speakers)
– Secondary storage (such as DVD/CD reader/writer).

Hard drive

Random access memory

There are also internal components such as the following.

– Random access memory (RAM)

– Read only memory (ROM)

– Internal hard drive

– Central processing unit (CPU) or microprocessor.

> These are covered in several sections of chapter 11.

Key Point	The CPU interprets and executes commands from the computer hardware and software; it is now usually on a single integrated circuit.

Software is usually of two types.

– Systems software which are programs that allow the hardware to run properly (for example, operating systems)
– Applications software which are programs that allow users to perform specific tasks (for example, using spreadsheets and wordprocessors).

> Refer to chapter 11.

It is worth mentioning here that most input/output devices use buffers and interrupts to communicate with the CPU allowing efficient use of all devices and the CPU itself.

A **buffer** is a temporary store where data is held until it is ready to be processed. For example, data will be held in a printer buffer until the printer is ready to print out the buffer contents; a keyboard buffer will store key presses until they can be processed, etc.

> They prevent slower devices holding up faster devices.

Since input/output devices work more slowly than the CPU, buffers allow the data to be stored until it can be processed (for example, printed) enabling the CPU to do other tasks in the meantime.

Also refer to chapter 12.

Key Point Buffers compensate for the different operational speeds of the various components that make up a typical computer system.

Interrupts also allow for more efficient operation of a computer system. A device will send an interrupt signal to the CPU indicating that it needs attention (for example, a printer is out of paper or out of ink and a CD is almost full). The CPU will suspend what it is doing to service the interrupt and then return to its task once the problem is cleared.

Interrupts can also be generated by software, for example, division by zero and out of data error – these interrupts again will need to be serviced and the system cannot return to normal until the issue is resolved.

2 Computer applications

In this chapter you will learn about:

- *Computer interfaces*
- *Communication systems*
- *Monitoring and control of processes*
- *Robotics*

The applications discussed in this chapter are by no means the only ones that exist, but have been chosen for their diversity and also to reflect the wide range of special applications now available to the individual and to industry. You will learn about how these applications work and their advantages and disadvantages.

2.1 Computer interfaces

To permit any application to work effectively, there needs to be an interface which is user friendly and generally easy to use. This section outlines the two main types of interface that the reader will normally encounter.

Command line interface (CLI)

In this method, the user has to type in instructions to open an application, choose something from a menu and so on. Frequently, a number of instructions are required to carry out a single task such as open or launch an application. This tends to be very slow, prone to errors and the user has to have some computer knowledge. The advantage is that the user is in direct communication with the computer which gives them greater flexibility than the next type of user interface.

Example of CLI: *c:\my program files\graphs\graphs.exe*

This would open and launch an application called *graphs* when typed in by the user. Some CLI instructions can run to several lines of text.

> Some of the many ways of capturing data (manually and automatically) are discussed in depth in chapter 10.

Graphical user interface (GUI)

In this method, the user is allowed to interact with the computer by using pictures known as *icons*.

This avoids the need to know where the application resides in your computer and involves simply clicking on the icon (using a mouse usually) rather than having to type in a set of instructions. Thus, the CLI instruction above could be represented by a single *graphs* icon.

Example of GUIs includes the **WIMP environment (windows, icons, menu and pointing device)**. Here each application to be opened is called a **window**. An icon from the windows environment is selected using a pointing device (for example, mouse) and this opens and runs the application.

> **Key Point** **Modern systems are capable of allowing several windows and applications to be opened at the same time.**

The following is a screen shot showing several windows (applications) open.

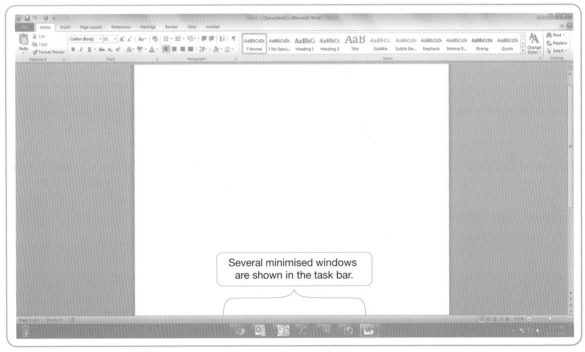

Several minimised windows are shown in the task bar.

Several minimised windows

2.2 Communication systems

A microprocessor is basically a computer processor on a single chip.

There are many ways in which computer systems or microprocessors are used in methods of communication. The four most common computer- or microprocessor-based communication methods are discussed in the following pages.

Electronic mail

A very common way of communicating is via *electronic mail (email).* This has some advantages over video conferencing in that you can read emails whenever you like (which overcomes time zone differences) and also the equipment needed is nothing more than a computer and a modem link. It also has obvious advantages when compared to traditional mail; i.e. it is faster to deliver the email (and get a reply) and you need not leave your house or office to send the email (very useful if you are disabled, elderly or even just very busy).

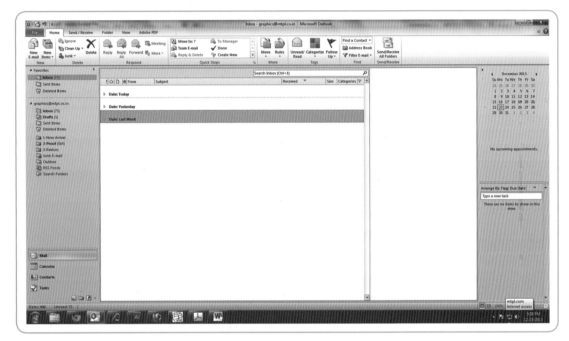

An email page

Frequently, emails are sent with *attachments*. There are a number of issues associated with this.

- If the attachment is large, it takes a long time to download and upload and in some cases may not open due to its size.
- It is possible to send viruses through attachments.
- It is possible that the recipient does not have the necessary software to open the attachment.
- The attached file may become corrupted during data transmission.

> **Other aspects of security are covered in chapter 4.**

So what happens when an email is sent?

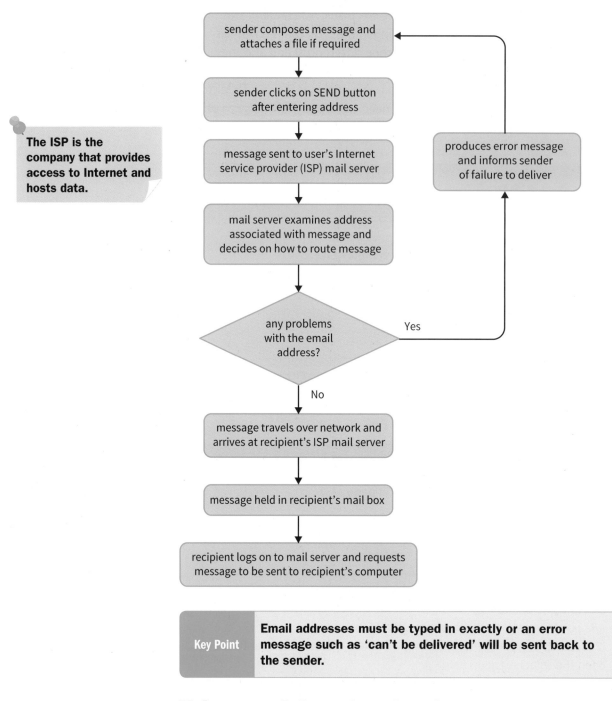

The ISP is the company that provides access to Internet and hosts data.

Key Point	**Email addresses must be typed in exactly or an error message such as 'can't be delivered' will be sent back to the sender.**

Voice over Internet protocol

This is a system that allows a user to talk to another user using the Internet. The user has three options.

computer ←——→ computer

computer ←——→ mobile phone

computer ←——→ landline phone

The user can either plug in a compatible telephone (via one of the USB ports) or use a headset to allow audio communication to take place over the Internet. The main advantage of this is cost; for example, option 1 (computer to computer) is essentially free. In option 2 (computer to mobile phone) the costs are in many cases 90 per cent less than with mobile to mobile.

The main disadvantages are:

- the caller needs to have a broadband connection and computer
- sound quality can be poor (drop out, echoes, etc.).

> Universal serial bus (USB) is a standard for connection, communication and power supply between two electronic devices.

Touch screens on mobile phones

Mobile phones are another very common form of communication. They are mentioned here since many of them now have features only found previously in a computer system, such as touch screens.

There are three basic types of touch screen technologies used by mobile phone manufacturers.

- Resistive
- Capacitive
- Infra red.

The following diagram compares these three technologies by describing how they work and what are the relative advantages and disadvantages of each method.

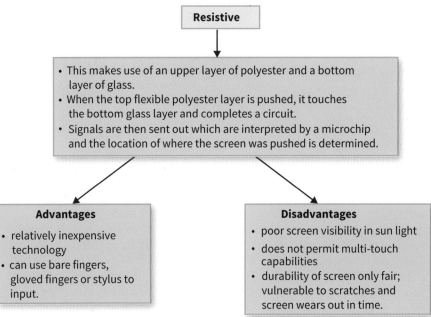

Resistive

- This makes use of an upper layer of polyester and a bottom layer of glass.
- When the top flexible polyester layer is pushed, it touches the bottom glass layer and completes a circuit.
- Signals are then sent out which are interpreted by a microchip and the location of where the screen was pushed is determined.

Advantages

- relatively inexpensive technology
- can use bare fingers, gloved fingers or stylus to input.

Disadvantages

- poor screen visibility in sun light
- does not permit multi-touch capabilities
- durability of screen only fair; vulnerable to scratches and screen wears out in time.

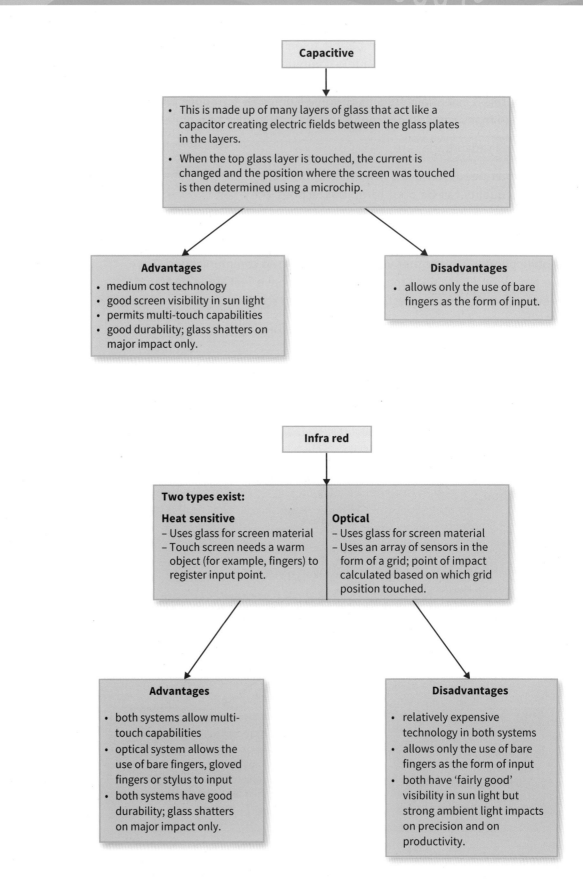

Capacitive

- This is made up of many layers of glass that act like a capacitor creating electric fields between the glass plates in the layers.
- When the top glass layer is touched, the current is changed and the position where the screen was touched is then determined using a microchip.

Advantages
- medium cost technology
- good screen visibility in sun light
- permits multi-touch capabilities
- good durability; glass shatters on major impact only.

Disadvantages
- allows only the use of bare fingers as the form of input.

Infra red

Two types exist:

Heat sensitive	**Optical**
– Uses glass for screen material – Touch screen needs a warm object (for example, fingers) to register input point.	– Uses glass for screen material – Uses an array of sensors in the form of a grid; point of impact calculated based on which grid position touched.

Advantages
- both systems allow multi-touch capabilities
- optical system allows the use of bare fingers, gloved fingers or stylus to input
- both systems have good durability; glass shatters on major impact only.

Disadvantages
- relatively expensive technology in both systems
- allows only the use of bare fingers as the form of input
- both have 'fairly good' visibility in sun light but strong ambient light impacts on precision and on productivity.

2.3 Monitoring and control of processes

Computers use devices known as *sensors* to gather information from the outside world. Since most information gathered is *analogue* in nature (i.e. constantly varying with no discrete values) it has to be converted using an *analogue to digital converter (ADC)* into *digital* data to enable the computer to understand and process the data. When controlling devices such as pumps, valves, heaters, etc. signals from the computer need to be converted back into analogue form (for example, electric signals) a *digital to analogue converter (DAC) is used*.

> Digital refers to the discrete data made up from the binary values 0 and 1.

| Key Point | Many monitoring and control applications do not use a computer system; a microprocessor is used instead but the methodology and the outcome are the same. |

There are many applications that use sensors. The following table shows which sensors are used in a number of common applications.

Sensor type	Possible applications
temperature	→ used in controlling central heating systems → used to control/monitor temperatures in a chemical process
moisture/ humidity	→ control or monitor moisture levels in the soil in a greenhouse → control or monitor the humidity levels in the air in a greenhouse → monitor the dampness/humidity in the air in an industrial process or application
oxygen/ carbon dioxide	→ environment monitoring (for example, measuring the oxygen content in a river to check for pollution) → measure carbon dioxide levels in a greenhouse
light	→ monitoring the light levels in a greenhouse → in a dark room monitoring for light levels → automatic doors to detect the presence of a person
infra red	→ detecting an intruder by the breaking of an infra red beam → counting things (every time the beam is broken it counts as one)
pressure	→ detecting intruders in a burglar alarm system → counting vehicles as they pass over a bridge
acoustic	→ picking up sounds (for example, footsteps when used in a burglar alarm system) → detecting liquids or solids moving in pipes/check for blockages in pipes

Sensor type	Possible applications
motion	→ detecting movement (as in virtual reality interface devices)
pH	→ used to measure acid/alkaline levels in a river (pollution monitoring) → used in a greenhouse to monitor soil acidity/alkalinity → used to monitor acidity in a chemical process
proximity/distance	→ these tend to be another name for the above sensors such as infra red, motion.
magnetic field	→ devices where changes in magnetic field occur (e.g. mobile phone or CD/DVD players) → used in anti-lock braking systems in cars/vehicles → used in traction control systems in cars/vehicles

The sensors are part of a system which is used to either *monitor* or *control* a process or application. There are subtle differences between the two methods.

Examples of monitoring

- Monitoring a patient's vital signs in a hospital
- Monitoring for safety in a chemical or nuclear process
- Burglar or security alarm (where monitoring for intruders is carried out)
- Pollution monitoring in rivers and the atmosphere.

Examples of control

- Controlling the operation of industrial process; for example:
  - Conditions in chemical reactions for safety and quality control
  - Nuclear power stations (maintaining correct conditions)
  - Production/reprocessing of nuclear fuels (safety and quality control)
- Controlling the temperature in a central heating system
- Controlling the environment in a greenhouse (temperature, moisture, soil pH, carbon dioxide/oxygen levels and so on)
- Traffic control (timing of traffic lights, etc.)
- Street lighting (controlling the switching on and switching off the street lighting).

In *monitoring,* the sensors send data/signals to a computer via an ADC. The computer analyses the data received and if it is 'outside normal values', it emits a warning and/or gives out some form of a readout on a screen or printer. The computer cannot change anything to alter the data being read by the system.

In *controlling,* again sensors are used to gather data and send it to a computer via an ADC. If the received values are 'outside the acceptable range', the computer sends signals to devices (such as pumps, valves, motors) to open/close, switch on or off, etc. so that the computer, in effect, is controlling the process. Consequently, the next sets of sensor readings are different.

Most industrial applications use **monitoring** and **control** since it is necessary to see what is happening in the process; but for safety reasons, the processes are controlled by computer systems as their response time is much quicker than humans.

The following flowchart summarises the key differences.

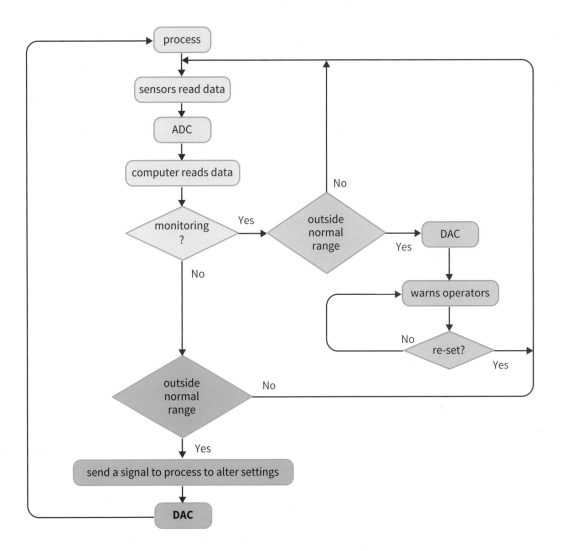

Let us now consider in detail **two** very different systems.

(1) Monitoring

Example 1 – a burglar/security alarm system

- gather data from sensors (pressure, infra red, motion) in the house
- signals are sent to an ADC where they are converted into digital
- the information is then sent to the computer
- the computer compares this information with pre-set data

DAC is used to convert signal to analogue so that computer can interface with alarm.

- if it is out of range (for example, pressure too high and beam has been broken) then a signal is sent to sound an alarm
- alarm continues to sound until system is re-set
- system continues to monitor sensors until turned off.

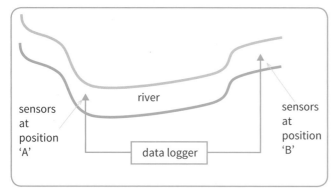

Example 2 – monitoring the pollution in a river

- sensors at position 'A' take readings (pH, carbon dioxide/oxygen levels and temperature)
- sensors at position 'B' also take readings to measure the same set of parameters
- the sensor data is converted to digital using an ADC
- the data is then stored in the data logger

- the collected data is downloaded every 24 hours from the data logger or is sent automatically via a communications link …
- … to a computer in the research laboratory
- readings from the sensors at position 'A' and position 'B' are compared by the computer
- the results are shown on a screen in the form of graphs, for example, or stored in a spreadsheet for further analysis
- the results from the sensors are also compared to data stored in the computer memory (for example, acceptable values or data readings taken on previous days)
- this allows predictions of pollution levels to be made or supply evidence that pollution is getting worse or better.

(2) Control

Example 1 – a chemical process which is temperature (must be 80°C) and pressure (must be 2 bar) dependent

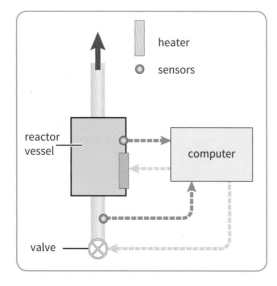

- temperature sensors and pressure sensors constantly collect data from the reactor vessel
- this data is sent to an ADC where it is converted to digital
- the information is then sent to the computer
- temperature reading is compared to pre-set value
- if temperature < 80°C a signal is sent to an actuator to switch on the heater
- pressure reading is compared to pre-set value
- if pressure < 2 bar a signal is sent to an actuator to open the valve
- DAC is used to convert signals to analogue to control heater and valves
- this continues until the chemical process is completed.

Example 2 – control of street lighting

- light sensors on the top of the lamp measure how strong the light is
- a signal is then sent to a microprocessor in the lamp body …
- … an ADC is used if the signal is analogue since the input to the microprocessor must be digital
- the microprocessor will contain 'light' values which are compared to the input data
- if the input is less than the stored value …
- … the microprocessor sends a signal to the lamp unit and the lamp is switched on
- to prevent the lamp keep switching off and on as light changes (for example, heavy cloud cover), the microprocessor will send signals to keep the lamp on for a pre-determined time duration
- after this time duration has passed, the data from the light sensors is again read within an acceptable range, the microprocessor sends out a signal …
- … and the lamp is switched off
- otherwise the lamp stays on for another time duration before it is checked again
- this monitoring of the sensors continues until the system is deactivated.

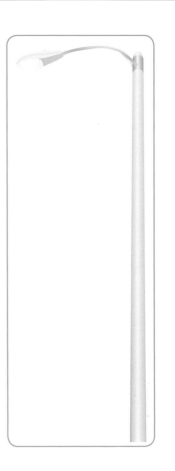

> **Note**
>
> Some street lights work using electronic clocks rather than using light sensors and automatically switch the lamp on or off at fixed times during the day. Since the on or off times are dependent on the time of year, a microprocessor is used to store these on or off times and it sends out signals to switch the lamp on or off. The microprocessor will check the actual time against the stored times (which will be different for every day in the year) and when a match is made, a signal will be sent out to switch the lamp on or off.

Why do we use such systems to monitor and control processes?

> Computers do not get tired or miss key data which could lead to an incident.

- It is safer due to faster response to problems in a process.
- Computer systems work 24/7 (even though human workforce can operate in shifts, key data can still be missed during, for example, a shift handover).
- Computers can take and analyse readings more frequently (for example, every 10 seconds which would be very difficult for a person to do).
- Computers are generally more accurate so there is less chance of misreading data.
- Computers have the ability to automatically display and analyse data without the need to transfer data (as would be the case when taking data manually.

Actuators

Actuators are used in many control applications involving sensors and computers or microprocessors. They are usually electromechanical devices such as a motor, relay or solenoid. Actuators can be digital (solenoid) but others require a digital to analogue converter (DAC) since the actuator needs an electric current/voltage to operate a motor or a valve, for example.

The use of actuators is mentioned in a number of applications in this chapter. The reader is advised to look at a number of applications involving sensors and actuators to find out some of the many ways these interact with a computer or microprocessor in a control environment.

2.4   Robotics

Robots are used in many industrial applications. They basically carry out the same functions as humans but have many advantages which will be discussed later. They are usually either linked to a computer system or have their own embedded microprocessor. Before carrying out any tasks, they are programmed by one of two methods.

(1) The robot is programmed with a series of instructions which allows it to carry out a set of pre-determined tasks.
(2) One of the skilled workers carries out the tasks manually and the movements/actions are relayed back to a computer; these actions are converted into instructions which are then stored in the memory. The robot is then operated under computer control copying the movement/actions of the human operator.

Robots rely on the use of sensors which continually gather data about its surroundings. Example is a car in the correct position to be sprayed with paint, is the paint spray gun empty, is there an obstruction in the way, is a part missing off a circuit board, etc. They are capable of doing some pseudo-intelligent tasks (for example, different sized cars needing to be painted) but in reality any non-standard routine is better carried out by a human operator. There are a number of advantages and disadvantages of using robots as discussed below.

Advantages

- Robots are capable of working in conditions which may be hazardous to humans.
- They can work non-stop, only needing a break when maintenance is due.

- They are less expensive in the long run since they do not need a salary.
- Robots are generally more productive (they can usually do a given task in a shorter time than a human).
- They are not necessarily more accurate than humans – however, the work that they do is much more consistent.
- They remove the need for humans to do boring, repetitive tasks leaving them free to do operations such as quality control.
- Less cost on factory environments – if human workers are absent from the factory floor then heating and lighting, for example, only need to be a minimum.

Disadvantages

- Robots can find it difficult to deal with non-standard situations, for example, a door missing from a car waiting to be sprayed; a windscreen about to be fitted to a car being cracked.
- They tend to reduce the need for human operators causing unemployment.
- Also since robots often take over the tasks done by humans, there is a risk of de-skilling within the work force.
- Since work can be done anywhere using robots, factories are often moved to countries where labour and operation costs are much lower.

2.5 End of chapter questions

2.5.1 Sensors are being used to monitor the environment in a greenhouse.

(a) What is the main difference between monitoring and controlling of a process?

(b) Describe how a computer and sensors are used to monitor the greenhouse environment; the temperature must be between 25°C and 30°C and the soil pH must be between 4 and 5.

(c) Name three other sensors and describe three different applications which use these sensors.

2.5.2 Robots are being used to spray some metal components with paint.

(a) Describe: (i) Two problems the robots might encounter when spraying these metal components.

(ii) How these problems could be overcome.

(b) In general, what are the advantages and disadvantages of using robots rather than using human workers in a manufacturing company?

2.5.3 A computer system has been set up with a graphical user interface and windows environment. Icons are used on the screen to identify applications.

(a) What devices could be used to select and open the appropriate applications?

(b) A command line interface could have been offered instead of GUI. What are the relative benefits and drawbacks of using both GUI and CLI to communicate with the computer system?

2.5.4 A mobile robot is used to enter harsh environments to take samples and to carry out maintenance work.

(a) The mobile robot is fitted with sensors.

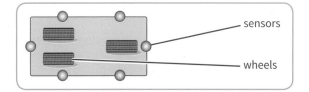

The robot is also equipped with an on-board computer.

Describe how the sensors and computer are used to guide the robot as it travels remotely. It needs to travel straight or go around corners without bumping into anything.

2.5.5 Name two types of mobile screen technology.

Give two advantages and two disadvantages of each of the chosen technologies.

2.5.6 A chemical process is being monitored using temperature sensors and pH sensors.

These sensors send data to a microprocessor. If the temperature in the process drops to below 50°C then a heater is switched on and if the acidity rises to a pH of 5, then a valve is opened to admit more acid (pH must be kept below 5).

Describe how the sensors and microprocessor are used to control the chemical process.

3 The Internet

Learning Summary

In this chapter you will learn about:

- *HTML*
- *The Internet*
- *Broadband and dial up*
- *Recent developments*
- *Intranets*

Studying the Internet is a large topic on its own. This chapter will deal with some of the key features and you will learn about website designing and how developments, such as social networking sites, have changed the way we interact and communicate.

3.1 The Internet

The Internet is a worldwide system of computer networks. It is possible to access any computer connected to this network provided you are given the necessary permissions.

However, what makes the Internet different is its use of *protocols* called TCP or IP (transmission control protocol or Internet protocol), which were introduced in 1974.

> The Internet was initiated in 1969 by a research agency in the US government.

Key Point	A protocol is a set of rules which is used by computers to communicate with each other across a network.

In reality, the Internet took off in the 1990s with the introduction of *HTML (hypertext markup language)* and *WWW (world wide web)*, which uses *HTTP (hypertext transfer protocol)*.

HTML (hypertext markup language)

Hypertext markup language (HTML) is a markup language and not a programming language. It allows the computer to identify a document's headings, lists, paragraphs and so on. Using HTML, a web browser would know how to display a document from a website in a way that makes sense to the user. It is easy to see the use of HTML when looking at the extension name in a URL since either *.htm* or *.html* would be shown at the end, for example:

http://www.programs.com/definitions.htm.

The following is an example of the use of HTML code when defining part of a document (the parts shown in < > are known as tags and the use of the '/' symbol signifies the end of a particular feature, for example, use of italic writing).

```
<html>
<head>
<title> This is an example of the use of HTML code </title>
</head>
<body>
<p> This shows you how the home page for a web page can be created in HTML </p>
<h2> HTML examples </h2>
</body>
</html>
```

HTML structure and presentation

When HTML is used, it is very important to realise that there is a difference between *structure* and *presentation:*

structure: this includes the semantics (i.e. the meaning) and structural markup of the document

presentation: this is the document style (i.e. how the document will look or sound)

It is important to keep structure and presentation separated throughout the design of the web page. Once the design is completed, the writer will end up with an HTML document (containing the structure and content) and a *css file* (cascading style sheet) which contains everything to control how the web page will be presented to the web browser.

HTTP (hypertext transfer protocol)

This is a set of rules for transferring files on the web (see example above); *http* was later developed to allow secured transactions on the web to take place. The http protocol works by transmitting the information using some form of encryption. In theory this should mean that the information cannot be accessed by anybody other than the user and web server.

Key Point	**Encryption is a process of transforming information using an algorithm which makes it unreadable to all except those possessing special knowledge.**

It is worth pointing out here the differences between the Internet and the world wide web (www) since they are often confused or regarded as the same thing. The Internet is the actual network itself; www is something which uses the Internet.

To view pages on the Internet, *web browsers* are used. The process can be summarised diagrammatically.

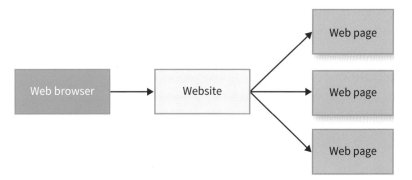

Search engines

They are a way of finding information (i.e. from websites and web pages) on the Internet. A user, however, needs to be very careful when carrying out such searches for the following reasons:

- not all websites are accurate (anybody can set up a website)
- it is possible to access 'unwanted' or 'dangerous' websites, therefore controls are needed to prevent access to certain sites
- the number of results (called **hits**) from a search engine could be massive.

Search results can be narrowed down by using AND, (+), OR, or quotes ( );
for example:

Type in CUP and the search engine returns ~ 284 million hits

Type in CUP+sample papers and the search engine returns ~ 817 000 hits

Type in CUP+sample papers+Geography and the search engine returns ~ 29 900 hits.

The order in which search engines display websites is based on a number of factors. Search engine optimisation allows typed key words to pick up websites. The success and popularity of certain websites is down to complex ranking algorithms used by the search engines. It has also been suggested that website ranking by certain search engines is revenue induced.

3.2   Broadband and dial up

Two common methods offered by *Internet service providers (ISPs)* for connecting a computer system to the Internet are:

- dial up
- broadband.

Dial up

Broadband

Kbps = kilobits per second

Phone calls can still be made even when the Internet is being accessed.

Features of dial up	Features of broadband
– this offers a fairly slower data transfer rate (typically ~ 60 kbps)	– this has a much faster data transfer rate (> 50 000 kbps)
– there is a need to dial one of the numbers supplied by the ISP every time one wants to connect to the Internet; therefore, dial up is not on all the time	– there is often an upper limit on the monthly download/upload file size (typically 20 Gbyte)
– the ISP contracts are usually for a number of hours per month and if this is exceeded additional charges are incurred	– it has the advantage of always being on and it does not tie up the phone line
– another drawback is that the phone line is tied up while the user is accessing the Internet.	– allows systems such as voice over Internet protocol (VoIP), online chatting in real time, C2C (webcam to webcam) to take place effectively.

Sample calculation

Suppose an ISP offers the following broadband data transfer rates:

- 40 megabits/seconds **download** speed
- 16 megabits per second **upload** speed.

(i)   If the user wants to **download** 30 music tracks which are each 3.5 Mbyte in size, how long would this take?

(ii) The user also wanted to **upload** 40 photographs onto a website so that his friends can access the photos. Each photograph is 1.5 Mbyte in size. How long would this take?

These are the answers.

(i) 30 tracks = 30 × 3.5 Mbyte   = **105 Mbyte**
    40 megabits/second = 40/8   = **5 Mbyte/second**
    thus, time to download 30 tracks = 105/5 = **<u>21 seconds</u>**

(ii) 40 photos = 40 × 1.5   = **60 Mbyte**
    16 megabits/second = 16/8   = **2 Mbyte/second**
    thus, time to upload 40 photos = 60/2   = **<u>30 seconds</u>**

3.3 Recent developments

Wikis

'Wiki' means fast in Hawaiian. *Wikis* are a type of software which allows a user to create and edit web pages using any available web browser. They support the use of hyperlinks and have a very simple syntax (rules) for page creation. Example of wiki: *wikipedia*.

> **Contents of wikis should be treated with some caution since anyone can create or edit them.**

Social networking sites

These sites are designed to promote the building of online communities who in general share the same interests and activities. They are aimed primarily at the younger generation who like to share photos, videos, music, favourite foods and so on.

Sample login page

They are usually free of charge and allow the interaction of people. Users can add friends, post messages to each other ('write on my wall') and update their personal profiles to notify friends about their likes and personal information, for example, *Facebook*. These sites are expanding quickly and there are some recent concerns about their safety and security.

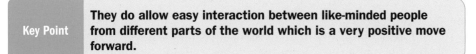

Key Point | **They do allow easy interaction between like-minded people from different parts of the world which is a very positive move forward.**

Blogs

These are personal Internet journals where a writer (called a blogger) can write some text about a topic or person; it is even possible to include links to certain websites. No real training is needed to create a blog.

Blogs can be day-to-day gossip (for example, my favourite rock star) to serious topics such as car safety issues, politics or even to organise a protest rally. However, it is still important to remember that comments made on blogs are still subject to the usual libel laws (which vary from country to country).

Web browsers

Web browsers are software that allow a user to display and interact with web pages and files from the Internet.

The software interprets the coding language of the websites and displays the *translation* instead of showing the *actual coding*. Consequently, a user can simply launch a web browser by clicking on the appropriate icon from the desktop and there is no need to know the commands which are required to interpret the website coding once it has been accessed. Every web browser has a screen toolbar with functions such as:

- go forward or backward to select previous sites already visited
- go to the first page since you first started to access the Internet during this session (known usually as the home page)
- save your favourite pages/websites for future use
- have the ability to view your website history.

Whenever a user clicks on or enters a *URL* (*uniform resource locator*), the web browser will request information (such as web page) from the web server selected.

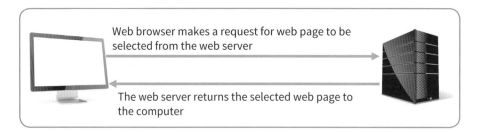

Web browser makes a request for web page to be selected from the web server

The web server returns the selected web page to the computer

The web browser will break up the typed URL into three distinct components. For example, imagine we had typed in: http//www.cambridge.org/computer_science_revision_guide.html

Then the three parts in this URL would be:

- the protocol (i.e. http)
- the web server name (i.e. www.cambridge.org)
- the file name (i.e. computer_science_revision_guide.html).

The web browser translates the web server name into an *IP address* which is used to connect to the web server. Following the http protocol, the web browser asks for file: computer_science_revision_guide.html.

The web server returns the HTML text for the selected web page to the web browser; this reads the HTML <tags> and shows the correctly formatted page on the computer screen.

Digital media sharing websites

These websites allow users to upload video files and other multimedia files for other users to access as required.

The video files are stored on the server and allows either free access to anyone or some form of code is required before the videos can be viewed. For example, *YouTube*.

Since most users do not have unlimited web space, this type of website is becoming increasingly popular as a way of storing/archiving a number of videos.

Internet service providers (ISPs)

These are the companies that provide the user with access to the Internet. Customers normally pay a monthly fee for this service.

Once a user signs up to an Internet service provider (ISP), an account is set up and a user name and password is created. Every time the user accesses the Internet this will be via their user account; it also allows the ISP company to monitor Internet usage.

> **A user name and password is required each time the user accesses the ISP from a computer.**

Podcasts

Podcasts are essentially a series of media files (audio and video) that are released at regular intervals and downloaded to a user's computer. Because of the method of delivery, this is a different way of accessing media files.

All of the media files are stored and maintained centrally and the listener or viewer simply employs the appropriate application software to access these files, check for updates and download new files in the given series.

Key Point	**It is possible to automatically download each episode/track of your favourite programme or artist as soon as it is made available.**

Tagging

Tagging is a type of *bookmarking* where a user *tags* a web page or photograph using some text to describe its contents. Anyone can view the web page or photographs corresponding to the tags.

For example, you have taken a photograph of your new car in 2010 showing Ipanema Beach in the background. Which folder do you place your photograph in so that you can easily find it again at a later stage? Tagging helps you resolve this dilemma. It is now possible to tag the photograph with key words such as: *my cars, Ipanema Beach, 2010*. So when you (or a friend) come to find this photo 2 or 3 years later, you do not have to remember where you stored it. Simply search on the tag and all the matching photos will be displayed.

Key Point	Tagging is essentially a form of 'bottom up' classification where there is almost an unlimited number of ways to classify an item.

Bit (data) streaming

This refers to data sent in a compressed form over the Internet that can be displayed in real time on the user's computer. The downloaded data is sent to a *buffer*; it is not saved on the user's computer and needs to be *streamed* every time the video or audio file is to be accessed.

Streaming...

Bit (data) streaming can be either true (i.e. real time) or on-demand.

True is when the information is sent straight to the user's computer and there is no need to save it first on the website server; the data is actually streamed live (i.e. in real time).

On-demand is when the files are first saved on a hard disk on the web server and played back to the user when they are requested.

There is a need to have a media player software on the user's computer that uncompresses the data and then sends it to a buffer before being played back on a monitor or through speakers.

Key Point	Buffering is an important component as it enables continuous playback to an acceptable standard.

The main advantage of this is that there is no need to store media files and it is possible to always download the latest version from the central web host.

However, if the buffering is slow or the broadband connection is slow, there will be delays in the playback which can be very annoying. Many webcams also use this method to send video data over the network.

Chat rooms and instant messaging

Chat rooms use instant messaging (IM) to allow communication in real time. A user registers with a chat room and chooses a user name and password that is to be used every time the user wishes to log in to the chat room.

Once they have entered the chat room, a list of people currently online will be alerted to them. To chat, the user types into a text box and may sometimes use **emoticons**.

The message becomes immediately visible to those online. It is possible to enter a chat room to read messages only and not contribute – this is known as **lurking**.

As a safeguard, users of chat rooms are warned about their language and use of the facility. It is important to prevent abuse, hassling other members, etc. and there is a code of conduct which, if breached, would lead to a user being blocked from taking part in the future. A controller monitors these chat rooms to ensure that any code of practice is not breached by the users.

Instant messaging (IM) is sending real time messages to another Internet user. It is similar to chat rooms but is generally on a one-to-one basis and is therefore, more private. Instant messaging is also a faster method of communication than using emails since it is in real time.

Interactive maps

On many websites (for example, hotels, shops, or general advertising involving the whereabouts of something) interactive maps are available. These usually show 3 options:

- road maps (conventional naming of roads)
- satellite views (aerial views of the area)
- a hybrid of both the above.

Satellite maps are a bit of a misnomer since satellites currently can only pick up something about 2 square metres on the earth surface. As you *zoom in*, at some point the satellite image is replaced with an aerial view showing the close details of the area.

The combination of aerial views and conventional maps is very useful since it gives users 'a feel for the area' (for example, is it built up, or are there any parks/green areas nearby?).

An example of a satellite/aerial view superimposed with traditional road mapping (option 3 on page 27) is shown below.

Satellite mapping

The most common features of interactive maps include:

- zoom in and out (shown as '+' and '−' keys on the map)
- the ability to move north, south, east and west (shown by arrow keys on the map)
- ability to get detailed directions from your house to the venue
- ability to use post code, street name or zip codes to do a search
- 'pins' to show exact locations of hotels, shops, etc.

Differences between IP addresses and MAC addresses

MAC addresses are discussed in some detail in chapter 11. A MAC (media access control) address is a unique number that identifies any device connected to the Internet. This address consists of the identity number of the device manufacturer (first 24 bits in groups of 3) and the serial number of the device (second 24 bits in groups of 3). The MAC address is very rarely changed so that a device can be identified no matter where it is.

However, each device using the Internet also has another unique address known as the **Internet protocol** (IP) address. This is a 32-bit number (e.g. 100.140.145.1). As soon as a device connects to the Internet, it is allocated an IP address and is unique for that session. It is possible to use the IP address to connect directly to a webserver instead of using the normal URL; for example: http://100.140.145.1

To summarise the differences between MAC addresses and IP addresses: suppose a user logs on to the Internet on Monday and then again on Tuesday:

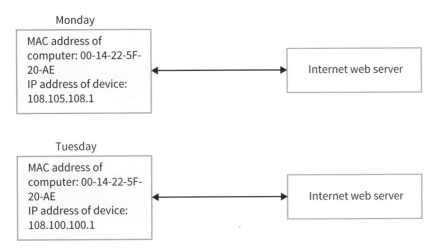

As you can see, the MAC address doesn't change but the IP address is different for both sessions.

3.4 Intranets

Many companies use intranets as well as the Internet. Basically, an intranet is a computer network (based on Internet technology) but is designed to work within the company only and is not available to users outside the company.

The main benefits of using intranets are summarised as following.

Advantages

- Intranets are safer since there is less chance of external hacking or viruses
- It is possible to have more control; for example, it is easier to filter out websites that you do not want your work force to access
- Companies can make sure that the information available to its employees is specific to their company needs
- If there is a need to send out 'sensitive' information (for example, security risk and data which could give competitors an advantage), it is easier to ensure that this information remains within the company.

A discussion of security aspects (both using intranets and the Internet) can be found in chapter 4.

The following shows a comparison of features found in intranets and the Internet.

- The term 'Internet' comes from INTERnational NETwork while the term 'intranet' comes from INTernal Restricted Access NETwork.
- The intranet only gives local information which is of relevance to the company and as it is easier to control intranets, it is possible to block access to certain Internet websites.
- Many intranets work without the need for modems; they can use a dedicated digital data transfer system.
- Since all the information on intranets are specific to the company, it is stored on central servers within the organisation.
- Intranets sit behind a firewall to further enhance their security.
- The Internet can be accessed from anywhere whereas intranets are only accessible to computers within the organisational structure.
- The Internet is available to anyone with a computer and the necessary software whereas intranet access requires passwords and user IDs just to gain access.

Refer to pages 32-33 of chapter 4.

3.5 End of chapter questions

3.5.1 (a) Explain the terms HTML, http and search engines in the context of the Internet.

    (b) Describe some of the problems associated with using search engines on the Internet to find information. How can these problems be overcome?

3.5.2 A company offers its customers both broadband and dial up Internet access.

    (a) Compare these two methods of connecting to the Internet.

The company offers the following Internet data transfer rates:

64 megabits per second **download** speed

24 megabits per second **upload** speed

(You may assume that 1 byte = 8 bits.)

(b)   A user wishes to download 80 music tracks which are 3.8 Mbyte each. How long would it take to download all the 80 tracks?

(c)   Another user wishes to upload 50 holiday photographs onto a social networking site. Each photo is 2 Mbyte in size. The user also decides to tag each photograph so that his friends can view his holiday photos.

  (i)   How long would it take to upload all 50 photos?

  (ii)   What is a social networking site?

  (iii) What are the advantages in tagging the photos on the social networking site?

(d)   Another user wishes to upload 20 videos showing motor racing events during 2011. What is the best way of making these videos available to all interested people?

3.5.3   Describe the differences between *digital media sharing websites* and *podcasts.*

3.5.4   Chat rooms are used by a number of people across the globe.

Describe:

(a)   What safeguards need to be in place to protect people using chat rooms.

(b)   How chat rooms work.

(c)   The differences between chat rooms and instant messaging.

3.5.5   A television company decides to offer customers the facility to view its programmes over the Internet. Customers will be able to get programmes through a technique known as *data (bit) streaming*.

(a)   The data (bit) streaming is offered as *true (for all live sports events)* and *on-demand.* Describe the main differences between the two methods.

(b)   Give the advantages of using data (bit) streaming rather than simply downloading video files.

(c)   Describe some of the problems associated with data (bit) streaming of video and audio files.

3.5.6   A company allows Internet and intranet access to all its employees.

(a)   What problems could exist in permitting access to the Internet?

(b)   What are the main advantages of using an intranet?

3.5.7   A user is buying a new computer and wishes to access Internet websites.

Discuss the software the user may need to access the Internet and to be able to communicate via text and sound.

4 Security aspects

Learning Summary

In this chapter you will learn about:

- **Security and data integrity**
- **Cookies**
- **Firewalls and proxy servers**
- **Secure sockets layer (SSL)**
- **Encryption**
- **Online safeguards**

The introduction of computers into all aspects of our daily lives has had some dramatic effects on our work patterns and the way we shop, do banking or book our holidays. This chapter looks at some of these impacts and also considers the need for protection to the individual and to organisations because of the vast amounts of personal information now stored and transmitted. Security has become a major issue in the twenty-first century and some of these threats and ways to overcome them or minimise their risk is discussed at length towards the end of the chapter.

4.1 Security and data integrity

Because this topic is continually changing the reader is advised to get regular updates from the Internet or from computer magazines.

There are several security issues associated with computer systems and many of these can lead to data integrity issues.

The following pages consider a number of potential security risks and each one has been split into four sections so that it is easy to compare their impact on computer systems.

The four sections used are as such.

- name of security risk
- description of security risk
- impact of risk on computer system
- safeguards available to remove or minimise the risk

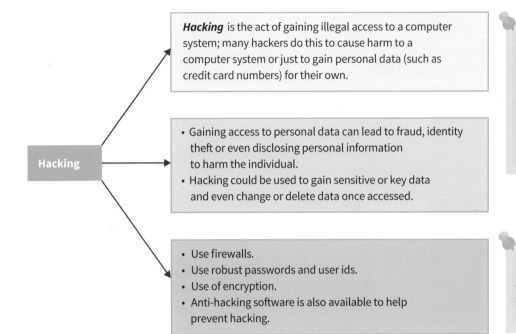

Hacking is the act of gaining illegal access to a computer system; many hackers do this to cause harm to a computer system or just to gain personal data (such as credit card numbers) for their own.

Hacking

- Gaining access to personal data can lead to fraud, identity theft or even disclosing personal information to harm the individual.
- Hacking could be used to gain sensitive or key data and even change or delete data once accessed.

- Use firewalls.
- Use robust passwords and user ids.
- Use of encryption.
- Anti-hacking software is also available to help prevent hacking.

Firewalls provide a log of incoming and outgoing traffic and can essentially prevent malicious access to a user's computer or block access to unwanted Internet sites.

Encryption does not stop illegal access to data but makes the intercepted data unreadable.

Another security issue, often confused with hacking, is called *cracking*. However, the two terms are actually quite different.

With cracking, the 'cracker' edits programme source coding so that the software can be used or changed to meet a specific purpose. More likely than not, this is done for a malicious purpose (for example, genuine software could be modified to perform a task such as pharming or spyware).

Hacking isn't necessarily harmful while cracking is always totally illegal and can be potentially very harmful.

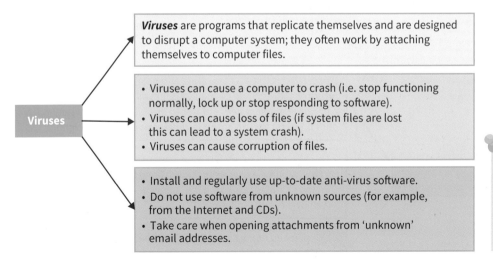

Viruses are programs that replicate themselves and are designed to disrupt a computer system; they often work by attaching themselves to computer files.

Viruses

- Viruses can cause a computer to crash (i.e. stop functioning normally, lock up or stop responding to software).
- Viruses can cause loss of files (if system files are lost this can lead to a system crash).
- Viruses can cause corruption of files.

- Install and regularly use up-to-date anti-virus software.
- Do not use software from unknown sources (for example, from the Internet and CDs).
- Take care when opening attachments from 'unknown' email addresses.

Anti-virus software detects and removes the virus or quarantines any files which have been infected.

Backing up of data may not guard against the effect of viruses since they may be attached to the files; deleting infected files and re-installing using the backed up files may simply put the virus back into your system. The only effective way is to install an anti-virus software and have it updated at regular intervals.

Viruses can be sent by emails, or as file attachments, or on a website which is then downloaded when the user visits it.

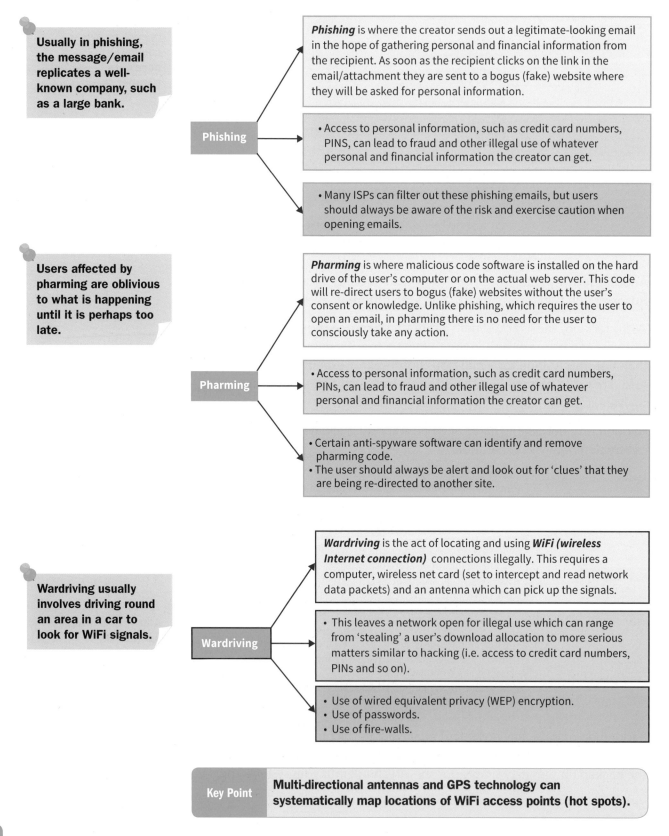

Usually in phishing, the message/email replicates a well-known company, such as a large bank.

Phishing is where the creator sends out a legitimate-looking email in the hope of gathering personal and financial information from the recipient. As soon as the recipient clicks on the link in the email/attachment they are sent to a bogus (fake) website where they will be asked for personal information.

Phishing

• Access to personal information, such as credit card numbers, PINS, can lead to fraud and other illegal use of whatever personal and financial information the creator can get.

• Many ISPs can filter out these phishing emails, but users should always be aware of the risk and exercise caution when opening emails.

Users affected by pharming are oblivious to what is happening until it is perhaps too late.

Pharming is where malicious code software is installed on the hard drive of the user's computer or on the actual web server. This code will re-direct users to bogus (fake) websites without the user's consent or knowledge. Unlike phishing, which requires the user to open an email, in pharming there is no need for the user to consciously take any action.

Pharming

• Access to personal information, such as credit card numbers, PINs, can lead to fraud and other illegal use of whatever personal and financial information the creator can get.

• Certain anti-spyware software can identify and remove pharming code.
• The user should always be alert and look out for 'clues' that they are being re-directed to another site.

Wardriving usually involves driving round an area in a car to look for WiFi signals.

Wardriving is the act of locating and using *WiFi (wireless Internet connection)* connections illegally. This requires a computer, wireless net card (set to intercept and read network data packets) and an antenna which can pick up the signals.

Wardriving

• This leaves a network open for illegal use which can range from 'stealing' a user's download allocation to more serious matters similar to hacking (i.e. access to credit card numbers, PINs and so on).

• Use of wired equivalent privacy (WEP) encryption.
• Use of passwords.
• Use of fire-walls.

Key Point — **Multi-directional antennas and GPS technology can systematically map locations of WiFi access points (hot spots).**

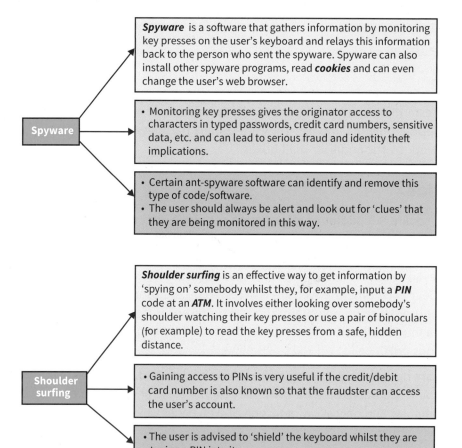

Spyware is a software that gathers information by monitoring key presses on the user's keyboard and relays this information back to the person who sent the spyware. Spyware can also install other spyware programs, read *cookies* and can even change the user's web browser.

- Monitoring key presses gives the originator access to characters in typed passwords, credit card numbers, sensitive data, etc. and can lead to serious fraud and identity theft implications.

- Certain ant-spyware software can identify and remove this type of code/software.
- The user should always be alert and look out for 'clues' that they are being monitored in this way.

Banks try to overcome this risk by asking a user to input characters from a password using *drop down boxes* (thus eliminating key presses).

Shoulder surfing is an effective way to get information by 'spying on' somebody whilst they, for example, input a *PIN* code at an *ATM*. It involves either looking over somebody's shoulder watching their key presses or use a pair of binoculars (for example) to read the key presses from a safe, hidden distance.

- Gaining access to PINs is very useful if the credit/debit card number is also known so that the fraudster can access the user's account.

- The user is advised to 'shield' the keyboard whilst they are typing a PIN into it.

4.2 Other ways data can be lost or corrupted

Certain other ways data can be lost or corrupted are considered below.

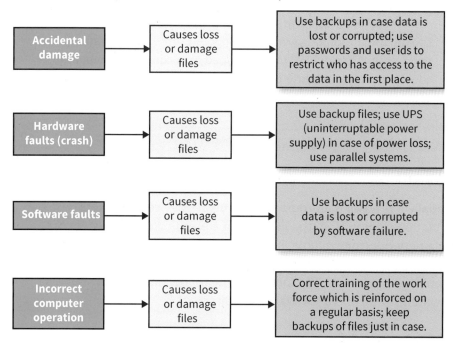

4.3 Spam and cookies

> Many ISPs can filter out spam or any other apparently unwanted emails; the user just has to be careful not to miss legitimate emails blocked by over-zealous ISPs.

Spam

Spam is essentially 'junk mail' sent out by companies or individuals to target people on a mailing list. They are usually harmless and simply 'clog up' network traffic and user mail boxes.

Cookies

An http *cookie* is a packet of information sent by a web server to a web browser and then sent back by the web browser to the web server every time it accesses it. Cookies are used to authenticate the user (for example, messages such as: 'Welcome Nicolae. If you are not Nicolae please log out' appear each time the website is accessed by the user). Cookies also carry out user tracking and maintain user preferences (for example, when visiting a music website, a user's music choice will be known as soon as he/she logs on).

Cookies are not programs but are simply pieces of data and are unable to perform any operations on their own. They cannot erase or read data on the user's computer and only allow detection of web pages viewed by the user on a particular website.

Although this information is used to form an *anonymous profile* of the user, and do not contain personal data such as name and address, they have been the subject of some privacy concerns lately. For this reason, they have been included here in the security issues section of the textbook. Nonetheless, cookies have been the subject of many misconceptions over the years. For example, *none* of the following are actually true:

- cookies are like viruses and can do harm to data stored on a computer
- cookies are a form of spyware/key logging software and can access and transmit personal data when typed on a computer keyboard
- cookies generate website pop ups/pop unders
- cookies are a form of spam.

4.4 Firewalls and proxy servers

Firewall

Essentially a *firewall* is a program or hardware device that filters information coming from the Internet to a user's computer system or private network (for example, intranet). It actually sits at the gateway between two networks, one private (for example, an intranet) and one public (for example, the Internet). The following diagram shows a hardware firewall and a software firewall.

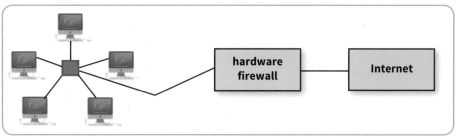

In the hardware version of the firewall it is usually connected to the IP router. In the software version, the firewall is stored on one of the computers which connects to the Internet.

Hardware firewall

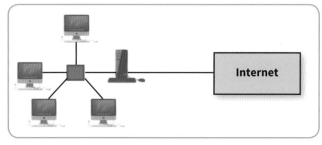

Software firewall

A firewall will carry out the following tasks.

- Examine all the traffic routed between the private network and public network ...
- ... and check whether the traffic meets certain criteria
- if the criteria fails, the firewall will block the traffic
- it filters inbound and outbound traffic
- it can be used to log all attempts to enter a private network and warn off such attempts
- can prevent access to undesirable websites or websites which pose a security risk
- it helps to prevent malware/viruses getting into computers on the private network
- it keeps a list of undesirable websites or IP addresses.

Proxy servers

Proxy servers connect users to the main website server and act as an intermediate.

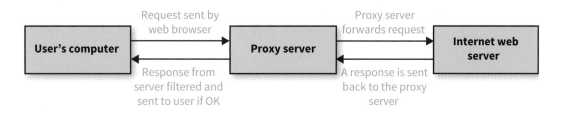

The features of proxy servers include the following.

- Proxy servers allow filtering of Internet traffic and can block access to certain websites
- proxy servers help to speed up the access of information from web servers by using a *cache*; the website home page is saved on the proxy server cache (part of its memory area) after it is accessed for the first time – the next time the user wants to visit the same website, it is now accessed from the proxy server cache rather than from the remote web server; thus giving faster access
- proxy servers help to keep a user's IP address anonymous thus improving Internet security
- some proxy servers can act as a firewall improving security from, for example, hacking.

4.5   Secure sockets layer (SSL)

Secure sockets layer (SSL) is a secure protocol developed for sending information/data securely over the Internet. It is often used when a user logs into a website as a secure area of that website.

SSL encrypts the data being transmitted; only the user's computer and the secure web server are able to view the data being transmitted. Obviously this is important when carrying out operations like online shopping so that personal details, such as credit card data, are kept secure. As pointed out in chapter 4, when the user goes to a website starting with **https**, the 's' indicates a secure website. These websites often use SSL certificates to verify their authenticity. So what happens when a user wishes to access a secure website and share some data?

- The web browser attempts to connect to a website which is secured with SSL
- the web browser requests the web server to identify itself
- the web server sends the web browser a copy of its SSL certificate
- the web browser checks whether the SSL certificate is authentic/ trustworthy; if it checks out as OK then the web browser sends a message back to the web server
- the web server will then send back some form of acknowledgement to allow the SSL encrypted session to begin
- the encrypted data is then shared securely between the web browser and the web server.

4.6 Transport layer security (TLS)

Transport layer security (TLS) is very similar to SSL as discussed in 4.5.

TLS is a more modern security system with some useful additional features. It is a form of protocol that ensures the privacy/security of data between communicating devices; in particular, when sending data over the Internet.

TLS is designed to prevent a third party hacking into Internet communications and is formed of two layers:

record protocol – this contains the data being transferred over the Internet

handshake protocol – this allows the website and user to authenticate each other and make use of encryption algorithms (giving a secure session)

Many older web browsers only support SSL, which is why both systems are currently in use.

The main advantages of TLS compared to SSL are:

- TLS allows new authentication methods to be added at a later date where necessary
- TLS allows session caching which improves overall performance (every time TLS or SSL sessions start, complex encryption keys are used which slows down the system; caching allows an existing session to be resumed thus increasing the efficiency of the security process)
- TLS separates handshaking from record protocols which improves the security of the system.

4.7 Encryption

Symmetric encryption

With *symmetric encryption*, a secret key is used which can be a number or letters. This key can then be applied to the message to change its content and essentially make it unreadable unless the secret key is also known. As long as the sender and recipient know this secret key, they can encrypt and decrypt all messages that use that particular key.

Obviously, the longer the key the more difficult it is for a hacker to identify it. For example, a 56-bit key has 7×10^{16} possible combinations which is actually quite possible to crack with modern high speed computers. The advanced encryption standard (AES) advises the use of 128-bit and even 256-bit keys to improve security; a 128-bit key has 3×10^{35} possible combinations which makes it considerably more secure – at least for the moment!

Public key encryption

One of the problems with symmetric key encryption is that once the key is known or cracked, a hacker can intercept and understand the message/data being transmitted. One more secure method is the use of *public* or *asymmetric key* encryption. This uses a private key and a public key. The private key is only known to the user's computer, while the public key is given by the user's computer to any other computer that wants to communicate securely with it. To decode an encrypted message, a computer must have the public key and the private key.

The sending computer encrypts the message with a symmetric key, then encrypts the symmetric key with the public key of the receiving computer. The receiving computer uses its private key to decode the symmetric key and then uses the symmetric key to decode the message.

Digital certificates are used to implement public key encryption on a large scale. These certificates are unique code that indicates the trustworthy status of the web server (see notes on SSL).

Authentication

Authentication is used to verify that information comes from a trusted source. Encryption and authentication work together to further improve Internet security. Methods of authentication include:

passwords	– user name and password; when these are entered, they are checked against a secure file to confirm an authorised person has 'logged in' to the system – if either user name or password are incorrect, access is denied
pass cards	– pass cards contain a magnetic stripe (which contains security information) and/or an embedded chip (which often contains a PIN)
digital signatures	– digital signatures are based on public key encryption (which use a private key and a public key)
biometrics	– biometrics are a recent introduction; they rely on the unique properties of certain aspects of the human physiology:
	– fingerprint scans
	– retina scans
	– face scan
	– voice identification.

Plain text and cypher text

Plain text is information a sender wishes to transmit to a receiver. This is the text used as input into an encryption algorithm. The output after the encryption algorithm has been run is called *cypher text*.

4.8 Online safeguards

Encryption is used in many cases to protect against the effects of illegal access to data, i.e. to prevent the hacker from understanding the data that has been intercepted.

However, many banks, for example, go one stage further when operating online banking. They not only encrypt all data but also use some of the following.

1. Use of user codes which is often an 8-digit or 10-digit code unique to a user.

2. Input some of the characters from a PIN and some of the characters from a password. This method prevents a hacker finding out the password/PIN, since each time a user logs onto the bank they will be asked to key in different characters.

   In the example below, the user is asked to type in the 3rd, 4th and 1st characters from their PIN and the 2nd, 5th and 9th characters from their password.

3. Alternatively, the user might be asked to key in the characters from their password using drop down boxes. This method is a further attempt to stop spyware picking up key presses and prevent the password characters becoming known to the spyware originator.

Please choose the following characters from your password using the drop down boxes:

2nd Character ▼

5th Character ▼

9th Character ▼

4. The user could then be sent to a page which states *'You were last logged in on 5th August, 2011. Is this correct?'*
   This is an additional check to ensure that only the official customer has tried to log on to the user account. If the customer had not logged in on the date supplied then this would indicate a potential security breach.

5. The user might also be asked to confirm some 'memorable' piece of information (such as mother's maiden name, user's mobile phone number).

6. Many companies send out card readers which need to be used every time the customer wants to access their account online.

ORG Bank

Home

Please give the last four digits of your debit card:

Please insert your card into the card reader and enter your PIN. Then key in the 8-digit code shown on your card reader:

The bank's computer will then check that this 8-digit code matches with the 8-digit code produced by the algorithm stored in its memory and will only allow access if they agree.

Chip and PIN cards

Many credit and debit cards are now fitted with a chip as well as a magnetic stripe. This chip will contain information such as the PIN.

CUP Bank

1234 5678 9012 3456

03/10   02/15

Prior to chip, the customer was asked to sign the bill as authorisation for payment.

This system was introduced to further improve security when using the card to make purchases, pay restaurant, etc. The chip and PIN is a fully electronic system and is a form of *electronic funds transfer (EFT)*.

We will now consider a typical example where a customer has decided to pay for his meal at a restaurant using chip and PIN:

- debit/credit card placed in card reader
- amount to be paid is keyed in
- chip on card is accessed
- card validity is checked (i.e. expiry date, is card stolen)
- a check is made on whether sufficient funds are available
- customer is requested to key in PIN
- keyed in PIN is then checked against PIN stored on chip
- if the card is valid and the PIN is OK, then the transaction is authorised
- authorisation code sent to restaurant
- amount of money for the meal is deducted from the customer's account
- same amount is debited to restaurant account
- receipt is produced as proof of purchase.

4.9 End of chapter questions

4.9.1 **(a)** Explain the difference between a private key and a public key when encrypting data to be sent via the Internet.

(b) Describe what happens between web browser and web server when a user wishes to access a website which uses SSL certification.

(c) Describe three different types of authentication used as security methods when accessing a secure website.

4.9.2 **(a)** Explain how a firewall could be used to secure the data in a computer connected to the Internet.

(b) What additional features do proxy servers offer to Internet users?

(c) Describe what is meant by a cookie and discuss any potential security risks associated with the use of cookies.

4.9.3 **(a)** Name four potential security risks associated with connecting to the Internet.

In each case, name a way of overcoming the risk.

(b) **(i)** What is meant by the term *cookie*?

(ii) Why do websites send out cookies to customer's computers?

4.9.4 Describe how each of the following problems could occur and name a way of recovering from them.

(i) Data loss

(ii) Data corruption

(iii) Illegal access to data

4.9.5 A shopping mall offers customers WiFi hot spots (access points).

    (a) Describe the security risk to users of this WiFi system.

    (b) How can this risk be minimised?

4.9.6 Look at the following list and tick (✓) whether it is a security risk or not a security risk to a user.

Description	Security risk	
	Yes	No
spyware		
virus		
cookie		
phishing		
spam		
pharming		
RSI		

4.9.7 Explain why these statements are incorrect.

    (i) Using encryption prevents a hacker gaining access to computer files.

    (ii) Data Protection Acts prevent viruses being sent over the Internet.

    (iii) Spyware is used to watch somebody keying in a PIN at an ATM from a long distance away.

    (iv) Keeping back- up files will be an effective way of recovering from a virus.

    (v) Call centres are always an expensive way of giving customer support.

4.9.8 **(a)** Describe three ways in which banks help protect customers from hackers and spyware.

    (b) How do banks reassure customers that phishing is not a threat to their online banking security?

    (c) A customer pays his bill at a restaurant using a chip and PIN card. Describe how this system operates.

Chapter

5 Programming languages and programming

Learning Summary

In this chapter you will learn about:
- *High and low level programming languages*
- *Turtle graphics*
- *Programming concepts*
- *Data structures: arrays*
- *Databases*

This chapter will look at programming languages and programming concepts including the use of one-dimensional arrays.

5.1 High and low level programming languages

Computers are of little use without the appropriate software. To write this software it is necessary to use one from a number of programming languages currently available. Programming languages essentially fall into two categories:

– low level (such as machine code or assembly code)
– high level (such as Java, C++, Visual BASIC).

Low level languages are either written in **machine code** (i.e. binary values) or in **assembly code.** High level languages are more sophisticated and replace several low level codes by one statement, for example, INPUT X, N = X + Y, etc.

> Assembly code uses codes such as LDA, STA, INC, etc.

Compare the following two pieces of code which basically do the same thing (i.e. add together two numbers called num1 and num2):

```
READ num1
READ num2
Total= num + num2
```

High level code

```
SED
LDA  NUM1L
CLC
ADC  NUM2L
STA  RESL
LDA  NUM1M
ADC  NUM2M
STA  RESM
CLD
RTS
```

Low level assembly code

Both types of programming language have their advantages and disadvantages.

<table>
<tr><td colspan="2">**Advantages**</td></tr>
<tr><td>Low level languages:</td><td><ul><li>allows user to address computer memory/addresses directly</li><li>user learns how the computer works</li></ul></td></tr>
<tr><td>High level languages:</td><td><ul><li>usually close to English and are therefore easier to write and understand</li><li>they are portable</li><li>they are easier to debug and modify.</li></ul></td></tr>
<tr><td colspan="2">**Disadvantages**</td></tr>
<tr><td>Low level languages:</td><td><ul><li>slower to write</li><li>more difficult to locate errors and to modify the code</li><li>tend to be machine specific/dependent.</li></ul></td></tr>
<tr><td>High level languages:</td><td><ul><li>need to be compiled or interpreted before they can be run on a computer this can be a slow process.</li></ul></td></tr>
</table>

Portability means that they can be used on any computer and are not machine specific.

Key Point — **To allow a computer to perform tasks, programs/software are usually written in a high level language.**

However, the computer only works in binary, so some translation process needs to take place. The methods used to translate high level language code either make use of *compilers* or *interpreters*.

Compilers

- these translate all of the original high level code (called the *source code*) into machine code
- the whole of the source code is compiled in one go
- a stand-alone program code (called the *object code*) is produced
- a list of errors is produced at the end of the compilation process
- whilst the compilation process is itself quite slow, the object code produced will run very quickly
- because all the code is compiled, when any changes need to be made, the whole of the source code needs to be re-compiled.

Interpreters

- *each line* is decoded one by one and then *executed*
- *no* stand-alone object code is produced; the interpreter needs to be present all the time

- errors (if any) are produced at the end of each line and the program usually stops at that point until the correction is made; this makes it easier to develop new software
- whilst interpreting is faster than the compilation process, because no actual machine code is produced (i.e. each statement has to be interpreted *every time* the program is run), interpreted programs take longer to run than programs converted into object code.

Each statement has to be interpreted every time the program is run.

The following flowcharts compare the two methods.

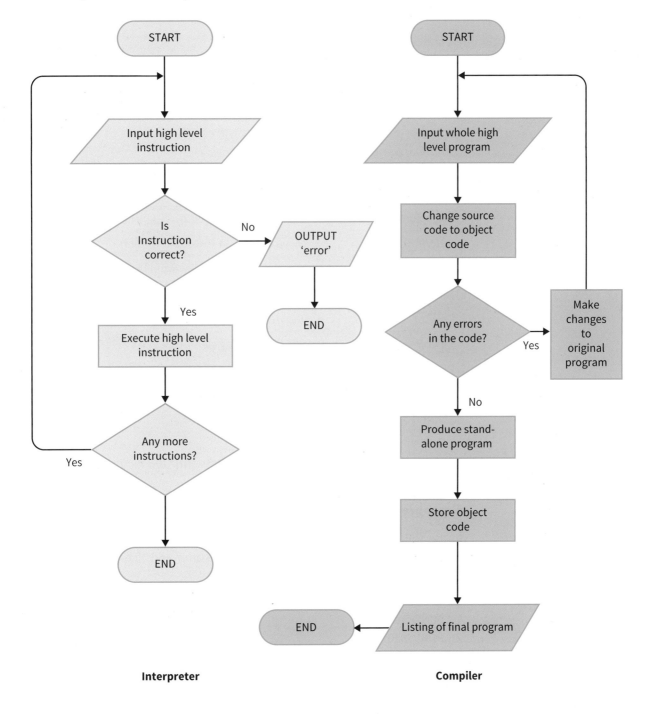

Interpreter   Compiler

An assembler is used to translate a low level language program into machine code.

Assemblers

– translate the original low level assembly code into machine code
– the whole program is translated and stand-alone program code (called the object code) is produced
– a list of errors is produced at the end of the assembly process

5.2   Turtle graphics

One high level language, known as *logo*, has given rise to a drawing application known as *turtle graphics*. A 'turtle' can be controlled by a number of on-screen commands; this traces out shapes of varying complexity.

The most common commands are listed below.

Logo command	Meaning of command
FORWARD *n*	Move *n* cm in a forward direction
BACKWARD *n*	Move *n* cm in a backward direction
RIGHT *t*	Turn right (clockwise) through *t* degrees
LEFT *t*	Turn left (anti-clockwise) through *t* degrees
PENUP	Lift the drawing pen up
PENDOWN	Lower the drawing pen
REPEAT *x*	Repeat next set of instructions *x* times
ENDREPEAT	Finish the REPEAT loop

To show how this works, consider the following two examples.

Example 1

In the following drawing, each square is 10 cm by 10 cm (and the diagonal is 14 cm). Draw the shape shown using logo commands from the above table.

The following logo commands could be used to draw the next page shape:

1 PENDOWN
2 FORWARD 10
3 LEFT 90
4 FORWARD 20
5 RIGHT 135
6 FORWARD 42

7 RIGHT 90
8 FORWARD 28
9 RIGHT 135
10 FORWARD 20
11 LEFT 90
12 FORWARD 20

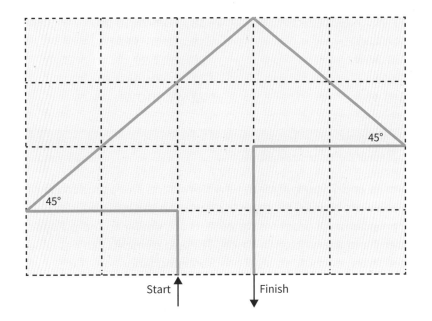

Example 2

This example shows the use of the REPEAT and ENDREPEAT commands.

Again, in this example, each square is 10 cm by 10 cm and it is required to draw the shape using the logo commands shown in the table.

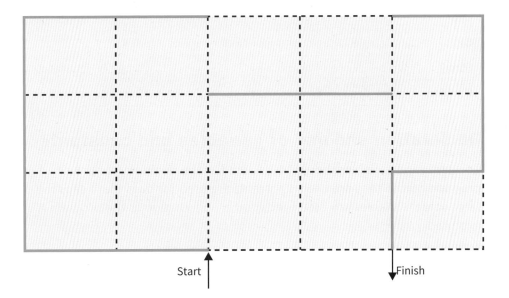

The following logo commands could be used to draw the above shape:

1	PENDOWN	7	PENUP
2	LEFT 90	8	FORWARD 10
3	REPEAT 3	9	LEFT 90
4	FORWARD 30	10	PENDOWN
5	RIGHT 90	11	FORWARD 20
6	ENDREPEAT	12	PENUP

13	LEFT 90	18	FORWARD 20
14	FORWARD10	19	ENDREPEAT
15	PENDOWN	20	LEFT 90
16	REPEAT 3	21	FORWARD 10
17	RIGHT 90	22	PENDOWN

5.3 Programming concepts

In chapters 6 and 7 you will learn how flowcharts and pseudocode can be used to solve problems. This chapter deals with the basic building blocks for writing programs. All program statements are similar to the pseudocode in chapter 7 and are written in Pascal. These statements can easily be replicated in any other high level programming language, see exercise at the end of the chapter.

Basic data types

These are the basic types of data that can be stored in a variable or a constant.

Data type	Description	Examples
Integer	whole number with no decimal point	1, 4, −1003
Real	a number that has a decimal fraction part	1.25, 4.00, −34.09
Char	a single letter, digit or punctuation mark	a, A, 7, !
String	a sequence of characters	table, 0678, Hello!
Boolean	only two values true and false	0 and 1, yes and no

Declaration and use of variables and constants

Constants and variables should be declared at the beginning of the program before they are used. Constants are used for data that keeps the same value; variables are used for data that will change as the program is executed.

Declarations

```
var firstnumber, secondnumber, total, count : integer;
var average : real;
var yourname : string;
var gender : char;

const myname = 'Helen';
const smallest = 0;
const male = 'M';
```

```
use

firstnumber := 100;
secondnumber := 200;
total := firstnumber + secondnumber;
average := total/count;
readln (yourname);
```

Programming statements

Assignment

Assignment statements are used to set a variable to a new value; for example, *start := 1;* or *percent := value / total * 100;* The new value can be set from a constant or an expression.

Sequence

A program consists of a sequence of statements that are executed one after another.

Selection – if statements and case statements

These are *conditional statements* in that some condition must be met before the next statement is executed. The format of each statement is:

```
if … then … (else) …
case … of …(else) … end …
```

```
if value = 0 then write ('zero')
            else if value = 1 then write ('one')
                 else if value = 2 then write ('two')
                      else write ('?');
```

```
case value of
  0 : write('zero');
  1 : write('one');
  2 : write('two');
  else write('?')
end;
```

Note that both pieces of code do the same thing – if value = 0, 1 or 2 then zero, one or two is output, if the value is greater than 2 then what is output.

Repetition

There are three common ways of carrying out repetition. All the following pieces of code carry out the same task: input 40 numbers and output their total.

The `while` loop is used when a condition must be met before the code within the loop can be executed.

```
count := 0;
total := 0;
while count < 40 do
  begin
    readln (firstnumber);
    total := total + firstnumber;
    count := count + 1
  end;
writeln ('The total is ', total);
```

The **for** loop is used when there are a fixed number of repetitions known.

```
total := 0;
for count := 1 to 40 do
  begin
    readln (firstnumber);
    total := total + firstnumber
  end;
writeln ('The total is ', total);
```

The **repeat** loop is used when the code within the loop must be executed at least once and the condition is tested at the end of the loop.

```
count := 0;
total := 0;
repeat
  begin
    readln (firstnumber);
    total := total + firstnumber;
    count := count + 1
  end
until count = 40;
writeln ('The total is ', total);
```

> **Note that the variables count and total need to be set to zero before use.**

Counting

Counting is a very common task in many programming languages: for example, *count := count + 1;* which means, in programming terms the value stored in the variable count is incremented by 1. It is possible to count in any increment required, for example:

```
count := count + 0.5; or count := count - 1;
```
                         (this is counting backwards).

Input and output

These commands input data into a computer and output data following some form of processing, for example:

read/readln (temp); and write/writeln (sum);

Predefined procedures/functions

Procedures

A procedure is a short piece of program code that carries out a task that will be used more than once. A predefined procedure is program code that most programmers will need to use and is usually available from a library of routines. For example, the library CRT makes procedures like `clrscr` (clears the screen) and `goto(x,y)` (move the cursor to this position) available to the programmer.

Functions

A function is a short piece of program code that carries out a task that will be used more than once and part of this task is to provide a value. A predefined function is program code that most programmers will need to use and is usually available from a library of routines. A function can be used on the right hand side of an assignment statement. For example, the library CRT has a function `readkey` which can be used as follows:

```
Value := readkey;
```

Making a program understandable

Programs need to be understandable to other programmers so that they can be altered or corrected if required. Here are some of the methods used to ensure programming code is easier to understand.

Indentation

All the programming statements inside a loop or as part of a selection are indented to make the code easier to read.

> For example, have a look at the code in Reading values into an array using a For loop.

Meaningful names

All the identifiers for variables, constants procedures and functions should be given meaningful names that show what they are used, for example, counter rather than `x` to count the repetitions in a loop.

Comments

These provide extra information for a programmer that is ignored by a compiler or an interpreter. Comments are added to make the source code easier to understand.

5.4 Data structures arrays

An array is a data structure that refers to a set of similar data items, usually of the same type, that have a common name and each individual item, called an element, has its own index. A one-dimensional array works like a list.

Declaration and use of arrays

Arrays should be declared at the beginning of the program before they are used. Declarations can include the size of the array and the type of the data to be stored.

Declarations

```
var index1 : integer;
var mynumbers : array [1..5] of integer;
var index2 : integer;
var mynames : array [1..5] of string;

use

mynumbers[1] := 7;
mynumbers[5] := 12;
mynames[3] := 'David'
```

Index variables in arrays

Each element in an array can be identified by its **index number,** for example, `colour[1]` is red and `colour[4]` is orange.

colour

1	red
2	blue
3	green
4	orange
5	yellow
6	white
7	black

Reading values into an array using a For loop

Data items can be easily read into an array using a `for` loop, the value for the array index is the same as the loop counter.

```
for index := 1 to 5 do
  begin
    readln (firstnumber);
    mynumbers[index] := firstnumber
end;
```

This programming is more efficient as there are often less lines of code required. Compare this program to find the average, and highest marks for three students without using an array:

```
var studentmark1, studentmark2, studentmark3 : integer;
var total, highestmark : integer;
```

```
var ave rage : real;
highestmark := 0;
total := 0;
write ('Enter student mark ');
readln (studentmark1);
if studentmark1 > highestmark then
highestmark := studentmark1;
total := total + studentmark1;
write ('Enter student mark ');
readln (studentmark2);
if studentmark2 > highestmark then
highestmark := studentmark2;
total := total + studentmark2;
write ('Enter student mark ');
readln (studentmark3);
if studentmark3 > highestmark then highestmark :=
studentmark3;
total := total + studentmark3;
average:= total/3;
```

With this program to find the average, and highest marks for three students using an array.

```
var array studentmark [1..3] of integer;
var total, highestmark, index : integer;
var average : real;
highestmark := 0;
total := 0;
for index := 1 to 3 do
  begin
    write ('Enter student mark ');
    readln (studentmark[index]);
    if studentmark[index] > highestmark
      then highestmark := studentmark [index];
    total := total + studentmark [index]
  end;
average:= total/3;
```

If there were more students, for example, 30, it would be easy to amend the second program using the array by changing 3 to 30 but there would need to be many more lines of code for the first program.

5.5 Databases

Databases

Databases are basically an electronic way of filing information to allow efficient storage, retrieval and cross checking of data.

There are several different methods used to structure the data in a database, but this is beyond the scope of this book.

However, it is worth highlighting the properties found in many databases:

Tables

Data is stored in rows and columns. Each row is known as a *record* and the data items are known as *fields*.

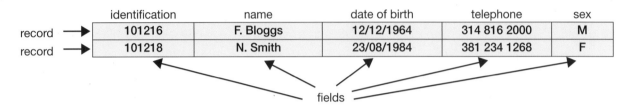

Each field in a record has its own data type. The data types in the fields can be text, alphanumeric, numeric, Boolean or date/time. In this example, the following data types have been chosen.

Field name	Data type	Reason for choice
identification	numeric or alphanumeric	Numeric – can be sorted on numerical order Alphanumeric – can be given a fixed length
name	text	Can be sorted in alphabetical order
date of birth	date	Automated checking provided by most database management systems, for example, the month must have values from 1 to 12
telephone	alphanumeric	Not used for calculations, can include other characters beside digits, for example, + ()
sex	Boolean or text	Boolean – only **two** choices M or F text – can have validation rules set for a single character restricted to the values M or F

Primary key

A *primary key* is a field that uniquely identifies a record in a table, for example the field 'identification' in the above table. The field 'name' would not be suitable as a primary key because the same name can occur more than once. A primary key must always be unique.

Queries

Queries permit information to be retrieved from a table. It also allows filtering so only the required records and fields are seen. Query-by-example is used to perform a search from given criteria.

Examples of query-by-example

Consider this section of a database table for **WORLD CITIES**:

	Name of city	Country	Continent	Population	Density	Area
1	Shanghai	China	Asia	13.9	7170	1930
2	Mumbai	India	Asia	13.8	22940	600
3	Karachi	Pakistan	Asia	13.0	3680	3530
4	Delhi	India	Asia	12.6	29150	430
5	Istanbul	Turkey	Eurasia	12.5	6210	1830
6	Saõ Paulo	Brazil	America	11.2	7380	1520
7	Moscow	Russia	Eurasia	10.6	9770	1080
8	Tokyo	Japan	Asia	8.9	14400	620
9	New York	USA	America	8.4	10450	790
10	London	UK	Europe	7.8	4860	1580
11	Bogota	Colombia	America	7.3	4570	1590
12	Rio de Janeiro	Brazil	America	6.3	5350	1180

Note the following:

- There are 12 records shown in this section of the database table and each record has 6 fields.
- **Population** is in millions, **Density** is per km^2, **Area** is in km^2
- If the following query-by-example was run

Field:	Name of city	Continent	Population
Table:	WORLD CITIES	WORLD CITIES	WORLD CITIES
Sort:			
Show:	☑	☐	☐
Criteria:		= 'America'	> 8.0
or:			

then Saõ Paulo and New York would be output.

The following query-by-example:

Field:	Name of city	Country	Density	Area
Table:	WORLD CITIES	WORLD CITIES	WORLD CITIES	WORLD CITIES
Sort:	Ascending			
Show:	☑	☐	☐	☐
Criteria:		= 'India'		<1000
or:			>10000	

would produce the following: Delhi, Mumbai, New York, and Tokyo in that order.

Note that the field names in the query-by-example grid should match up exactly with the field names in the database table.

Query-by-examples are constructed using a column for each field required, this contains the following information:

Field:	name of field in database table
Table:	name of database table
Sort:	ascending, descending or bank for not sorted
Show:	☑ show this field ☐ do not show this field
Criteria:	all the criteria for each field in this row are joined with AND
or:	use this row for OR

File maintenance

Files stored on databases need to be regularly maintained to ensure they are up to date and accurate. Updating usually involves *amending, inserting* or *deleting* of data. To show how this works, we will consider a hospital keeping records of its patients on a database.

An example of **amending** would be: updating telephone number, address, name (the patient may marry and change their surname) and so on.

An example of **inserting** would be: a new patient came to the hospital for the first time and a record would need to be inserted into the file.

An example of **deleting** would be: a patient dies or moves to another country

5.6 End of chapter questions

The next two questions require logo to be used to produce the two shapes shown. In each question, the squares are 10 cm by 10 cm and the diagonals are 14 cm. Use the following list of commands only to draw your shapes.

Logo command	Meaning of command
FORWARD n	Move n cm in a forward direction
BACKWARD n	Move n cm in a backward direction
RIGHT t	Turn right (clockwise) through t degrees
LEFT t	Turn left (anticlockwise) through t degrees
PENUP	Lift the drawing pen up
PENDOWN	Lower the drawing pen
REPEAT x	Repeat next set of instructions x times
ENDREPEAT	Finish the REPEAT loop

5.6.1

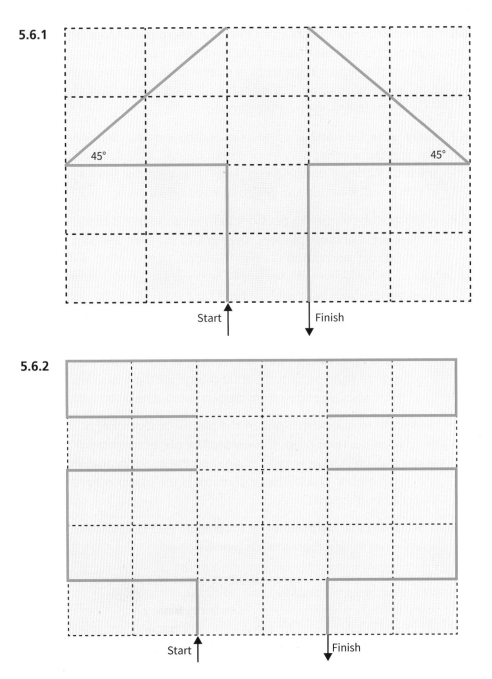

Start   Finish

5.6.2

Start   Finish

5.6.3 Using your usual programming language complete the declarations and statements from section 5.3 Programming concepts in this chapter. Add some code to input a value for the `if` and `case` statements and test your program with the values 0, 1, 2, 3 and 4.

5.6.4 Write a program using a `for` loop to input 10 numbers and output how many were over 20. Rewrite your program to use a `while` loop and then a `repeat` loop. Which type of loop should you choose and why?

5.6.5 Write a program to input the marks for 20 students, display and calculate the average and display the highest and lowest mark.

(Extension to question, each mark must be between 0 and 60 inclusive, any other values must be rejected with an error message).

5.6.6 Write a program that allows a person to store their name, age and gender. The age must be a whole number in years between 18 and 100 and the gender must be M or F any other values are rejected with an error message. The person is allowed a maximum of 3 tries to enter both the age and the gender.

5.6.7 Every week the number of hours of sunshine is recorded for each day and the number of centimetres of rainfall. Calculate and display the total hours of sunshine and the total rainfall for the week. Identify and print out any days that have no sunshine.

5.6.8 A sports club charges $5 per hour per person to hire a tennis court. If there are 3 or more players, there is a 25 per cent discount on the **total** cost per hour. A further 10 per cent discount on the **total** cost per hour is given if they book the court for 3 hours or more. (So 4 players booking the court for 4 hours would be charged $80 – $20 – $8, i.e. $52; 5 players booking the court for 2 hours would be charged $50 – $12.50 – $0, i.e. $37.50).

Write a program, which inputs the number of players and number of hours required and outputs the total charge for the hire of the tennis court. Hint: your algorithm from chapter 8 could help you with this.

(Extension to question: if one of the players is a member of the club, the charge per hour drops to only $4. The player and one of the staff at the club both have to type in a 4-digit PIN to verify that the player is a club member. The 2 PINs must match if the player is to receive his $1 per hour discount).

5.6.9 A database table has been set up to compare FREEZER FEATURES. A section of this database table is shown below:

freezer id	price ($)	lowest temp (°C)	capacity (m³)	warranty (years)	colour
A	300.00	−20	0.16	1	white
B	250.00	−18	0.15	1	silver
C	400.00	−22	0.25	2	white
D	300.00	−20	0.18	3	white
E	520.00	−40	0.35	3	silver
F	360.00	−25	0.30	1	white
G	410.00	−30	0.30	2	white
H	290.00	−18	0.20	2	silver

(a) How many (i) records
             (ii) fields
    are shown in this section of the database?

(b) Which field is the primary key?

(c) What items would be output from this query-by-example?

Field:	freezer id	price ($)	warranty (years)	colour
Table:	FREEZER FEATURES	FREEZER FEATURES	FREEZER FEATURES	FREEZER FEATURES
Sort:				
Show:	☑	☐	☐	☐
Criteria:			>1	= 'silver'
or:		>300		

(d) Complete a query-by-example grid to find all freezers which operate below −25°C and have a capacity which is more than 0.24 m³.

Field:				
Table:				
Sort:				
Show:	☑	☐	☐	☐
Criteria:				
or:				

5.6.10 A database table was set up to show various features of a number of HOTELS near an airport. Part of this database table is shown below:

ref no	hotel	no stars	weekday tariff ($)	weekend tariff ($)	no of rooms	km to airport
1	Grand	3	50.00	40.00	21	5
2	Northern	4	70.00	60.00	64	4
3	Western	2	45.00	40.00	20	8
4	Quality	5	100.00	75.00	150	2
5	Albion	3	60.00	50.00	40	15
6	Orion	2	35.00	25.00	32	20
7	Denver	2	40.00	30.00	20	15
8	Wellbeing	3	45.00	35.00	50	10
9	Classic	4	80.00	60.00	75	6

(a) How many records are shown in this section of the database table?

(b) Which field is the primary key?

(c) If the following query-by-example grid was used:

Field:	ref no	no stars	weekend tariff ($)
Table:	HOTELS	HOTELS	HOTELS
Sort:			
Show:	☑	☐	☐
Criteria:		= 4	
or:			>45

What would be output?

(d) Write down the query-by-example grid to find all hotels which are less than 10 km from the airport or have more than 50 rooms and a weekday tariff which is less than $100.

Field:				
Table:				
Sort:				
Show:	☐	☐	☐	☐
Criteria:				
or:				

(e) Write down the query-by-example grid to find all hotels showing ref no only, with the records in *ascending order* after being sorted on **weekday tariff ($)**.

Field:				
Table:				
Sort:				
Show:	☐	☐	☐	☐
Criteria:				
or:				

5.6.11 A company wishes to keep details about its employees who work in Europe using a database table. The record format for each employee is shown below:

Name:	Alphanumeric	20 characters
Sex:	Alphanumeric	1 character
Department:	Alphanumeric	1 character
European country:	Alphanumeric	12 characters
Number of years working in company:	Numeric	2 digits

The following codes are used in the records:

Sex: F = female
M = male

Department: A = administration
P = personnel
M = management
F = finance

Two records from this database table are shown below:

W	I	L	S	O	N		K							F	M	I	T	A	L	Y					0	7
P	H	I	L	L	I	P	S		K	G				M	F	R	O	M	A	N	I	A			2	4

(a) In which department does KG Phillips work?

(b) Show how you would store the record for a Miss M Majid, who works for the personnel department in Germany. She has worked in the company for 9 years.

(c) Give **two** advantages of using codes when saving data in files.

(d) Why is it NOT a good idea to store **No of years working in company**? What would be a better piece of information to store?

(e) Explain why none of the fields in this database table are suitable to be used as a primary key.

(f) Suggest a new primary key field giving name, data type and length and explain why it would be suitable to use as a primary key.

In this chapter you will learn about:

- *Structure diagrams, top down design, menus, library routines and subroutines*
- *Common flowchart symbols*
- *Problem solving using flowcharts*
- *Dry running of flowcharts (trace tables)*

In this chapter we will look at various uses of flowcharts and consider how to produce them and also how to interpret them.

Flowcharts are a diagrammatic way of representing a problem, a task or a sequence of instructions. When solving problems, they are also known as an algorithm.

6.1 Structure diagrams, top down design, menus, library routines and subroutines

These are sometimes called tree diagrams.

Structure diagrams are a graphical way of representing a problem showing different levels of detail. For example, look at the following example which shows items in a department store.

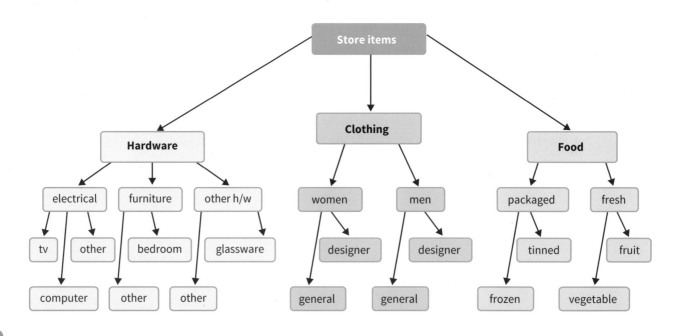

Note how each stage breaks down into increasingly greater levels of detail. This is a similar concept to **top down design** where a given problem is broken down into increasingly smaller and smaller tasks.

Key Point	**This method is frequently used to develop large, often complex, software packages where each 'chunk' of the software is written in the form of a module.**

These modules are all put together to form the main program. This allows several programmers to work on the same software package and makes testing easier since each module needs to be tested separately. Finally, the modules are linked and the whole program/package is again tested to ensure that there are no clashes between these linked modules.

This method allows for a very structured approach and also permits a **library of routines** to be used. This saves having to design the routines/modules each time (and therefore saves time and money) and they will also be fully pre-tested. Since the routines/modules may be used in many software packages, they permit compatibility (for example, passing of data between programs).

Library of routines are procedures, modules or subroutines stored in a 'library' which can be used in other software where required.

The only real drawback is that software packages tend to be much larger (taking up much more memory) and less efficient since the routines/modules may have a lot of duplication when compared to writing a single software package 'from scratch' – however, this would be a much slower and more costly exercise. The advent of modern computers with fast processors and large memories has allowed these programming techniques to become more common.

Menus make full use of structure/tree diagrams. Menus usually have some form of pointing device (for example, mouse) or a **touch screen** to select options.

In the example used earlier, the department store items could be in the form of a series of menus linked to several different screens.

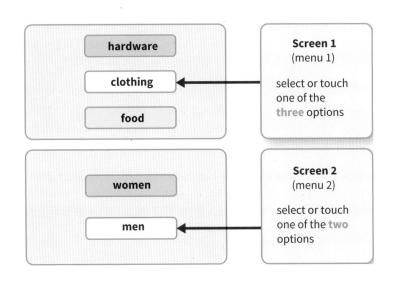

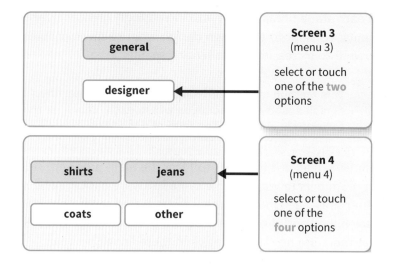

The menus could go one stage further offering price, colour, size or style options. Note that once *clothing* is selected from menu 1 the user is directed to another screen where a new menu appears. The user is directed to new screens and menus until the required level of choice is reached.

However, it is also possible to use *drop down menus*. This type of menu works where there are a **finite** number of options (as above) and they also prevent input of irrelevant data into the system. For example, choosing your date of birth.

> Here the user has chosen day 3, month 4 and year 1992.

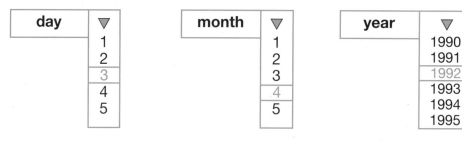

By clicking on the arrow, [▽], the menu options appear in a drop down box, and the user then highlights the value they want. The required option is usually chosen by clicking on a mouse. This is different to the menu options approach shown in the previous example.

With drop down menus, the possible menu options are shown in a box on the **same screen** once the user clicks on the arrow; whereas in the previous example, once a selection was made, the user was then **directed** to a new screen where the next set of menu options were shown.

Cascading drop down menus take the concept a little further. Using the department store as the example again, each highlighted option leads to another drop down menu and so on until the desired level is reached.

> The user 'drags' the mouse across to each drop down menu in turn until the required option is reached.

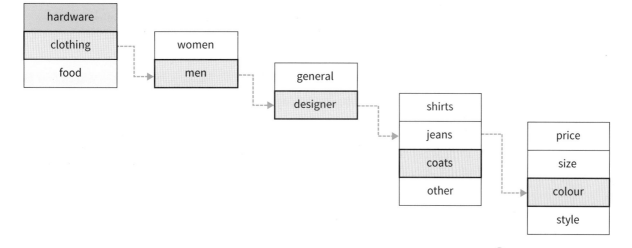

Cascading series of drop down menus show which item was selected (using a pointing device) from each menu. All the menu options are shown on one screen and the user 'drags' the mouse across to each drop down menu in turn.

> Note that the menu options in the next menu are only revealed after the user has selected an option from the previous menu.

6.2 Common flowchart symbols

We will first consider the more common flowchart symbols.

> Also refer to chapter 5 which considers systems flowcharts.

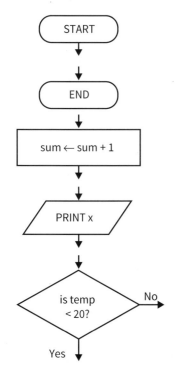

start box shows the beginning of any flowchart

end box shows where the flowchart terminates

process box shows calculations, summations, etc.

input/output box shows where data is input or output from the flowchart

decision box – answer to question in this box must always be YES or NO – no other options can exist since this only allows Boolean operators

Flow lines (↓) connect the flowchart symbols and show the sequence of the steps.

Key Point | **Most flowcharts can be constructed using flow lines and a combination of these five symbols.**

6.3 Problem solving using flowcharts

The following problems can all be solved using flowcharts. Each follows a logical series of steps; but no single correct solution exists, and the following are simply guidelines on good flowchart construction.

Problem 1

A garage sells cars. The amount of road tax is based on engine size. Engines over 3 litres in size incur a tax of $500, engines over 2 litres in size incur a tax of $300 and engines over 1 litre in size are taxed at the rate of $100. Cars with engines below 1 litre incur no road tax. Write an algorithm, in the form of a flowchart, to show the tax due on any car sold by the garage.

Solution

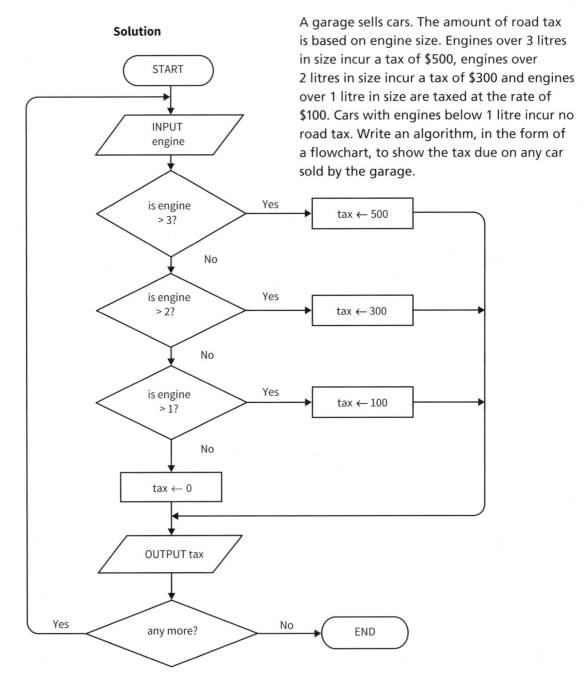

Problem 2

The heights of 500 students in a school are being measured. Write an algorithm, in the form of a flowchart, which inputs all 500 heights and outputs how many students were taller than 1.45 metres or shorter than 1.45 metres.

Solution

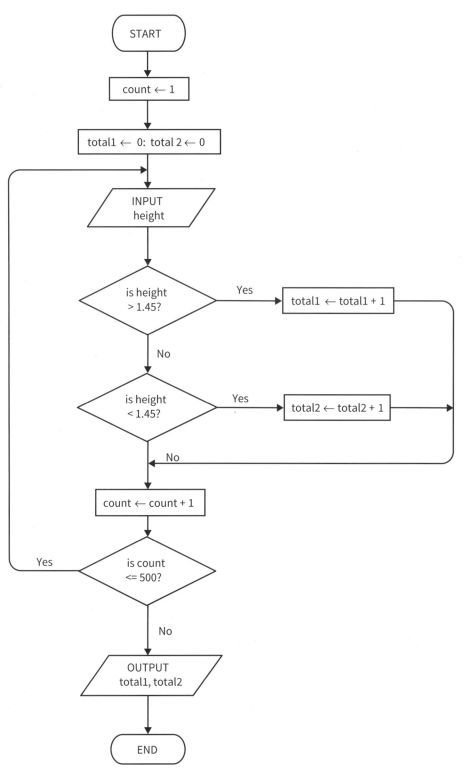

Problem 3

Write an algorithm, in the form of a flowchart, which:

- inputs the weight of 1000 items
- outputs the weight of the heaviest and the lightest item
- outputs the average (mean) weight of all the items input.

Solution

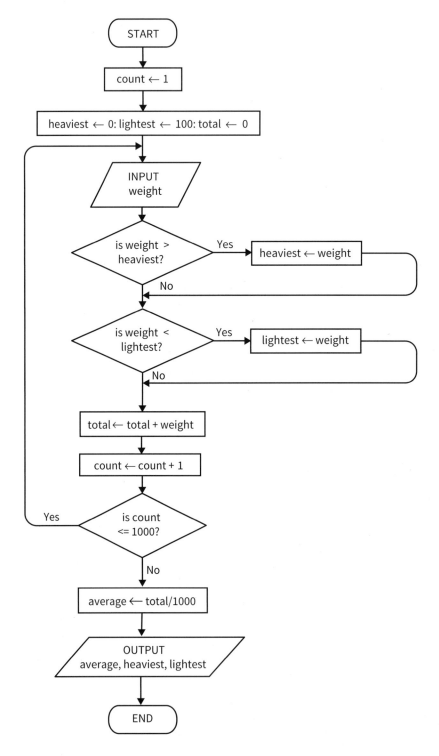

Problem 4

A small shop sells sweets, magazines and drinks. Each item sold is identified by a unique 4-digit code. All sweets sold have a code that starts with a 1, all magazines sold have a code that starts with a 2 and all drinks sold have a code that starts with a 3. So:

1000 to 1999 are the codes for sweets,
2000 to 2999 are the codes for magazines, and
3000 to 3999 are the codes for drinks.
(9999 is used to stop the algorithm)

Solution

Write an algorithm, in the form of a flowchart, which inputs the codes for all of the items sold in the shop and outputs how many items sold were sweets, magazines or drinks.

This is an interesting problem since it shows a clever way of finding a value.

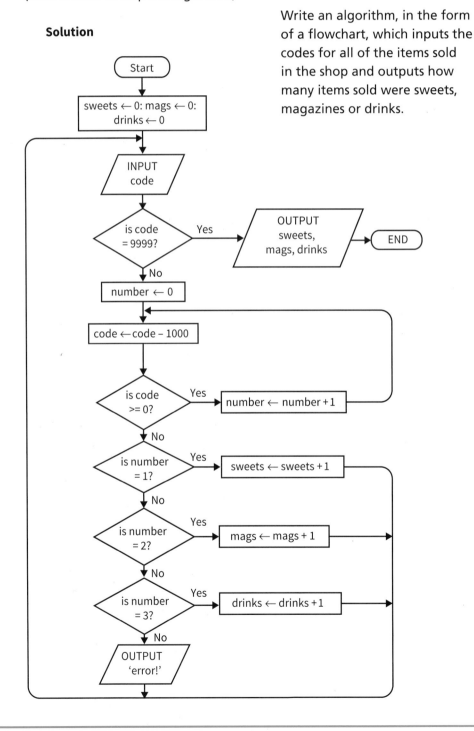

Solution

Problem 5

Some students have been carrying out 5 experiments; 20 temperature readings were taken in each experiment.

Write an algorithm, in the form of a flowchart, which inputs all of the temperature readings, and outputs the average (mean) temperature for EACH experiment, the average (mean) temperature for ALL 5 experiments and the highest temperature recorded from all the readings taken.

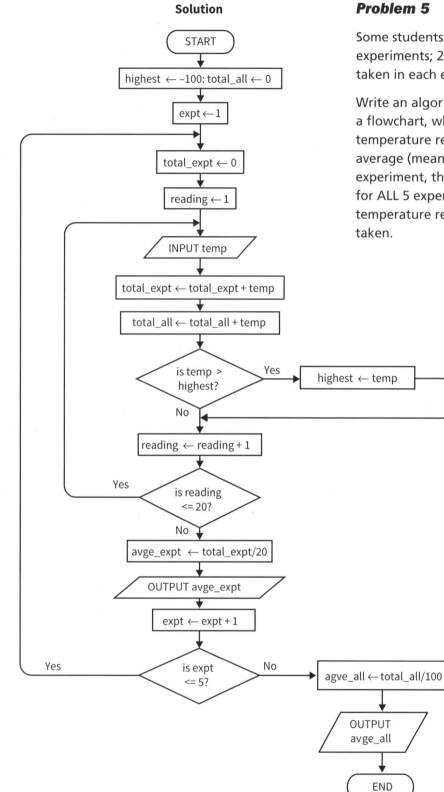

This problem makes use of *nested loops* (a loop inside another loop) since there are 5 experiments with 20 results from EACH experiment.

6.4 Dry running of flowcharts (trace tables)

Dry running of flowcharts is done to:

- find the output for a given set of data to test if the flowchart gives expected results
- check the logic of the flowchart
- find out what a given algorithm has been designed to do.

A dry run is normally done by a technique known as a *trace table*. This shows how the *variables* in the flowchart change at each stage. There are many advantages in doing this rather than just 'mentally work through the problem'.

Test data is used to test the logic of a flowchart or program. There are three types of test data.

Normal data

- to test for expected results
- the data used in example 1 is normal data

Extreme/boundary data

- data at the limit of acceptability
- the value −1 in example 2 is boundary data for the negative numbers, −1 is at the upper bound for negative whole numbers, 1 would be at the lower bound for positive whole numbers

Erroneous/abnormal data

- this data should be rejected and an error message produced
- for question 6.5.6, a time of 0 must be rejected as the calculation would not work with this value

---

Advantages

- If you make an error, it is much easier to back track in order to find out where the error is.
- There is also less chance of making an error using this method.
- It encourages students to adopt a logical approach and helps to determine suitable test data to check out a given algorithm.

When producing trace tables it is a good idea to use a new line for all the variable values whenever the flowchart loops back to an input, re-sets counts, etc. Example:

a	b	c	total A	total B	read X
0	0	0	0	0	8
1			8		3
2			11		
0	0	0	0	0	−2

The following three examples show the trace tables for a given set of data. It is advisable to go through each one carefully to see what the flowchart is doing and make sure you get the same output.

Example 1

This flowchart inputs three numbers which undergo a series of checks and an output is produced.

The following data is to be used: 42, 6400, −80.

Flowchart

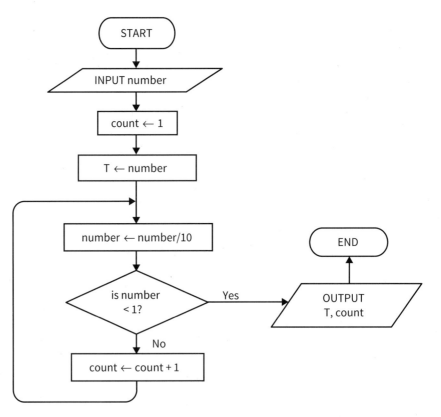

Trace table

number	count	T	OUTPUT T, count
42 4.2 0.42	1 2	42	42, 2
6400 640 64 6.4 0.64	1 2 3 4	6400	6400, 4
−80 −8	1	-80	−80,1

Example 2

This flowchart inputs 10 numbers and outputs how many were negative, how many were positive and how many were zero.

The following data is to be used: −1, 2, 4, 0, 0, 2, −3, 0, 12, 8.

Flowchart

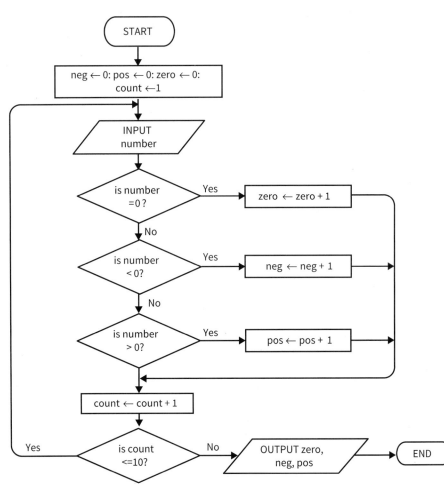

Trace table

count	zero	neg	pos	number	OUTPUT
1	0	0	0	–1	3, 2, 5
2	1	1	1	2	
3	2	2	2	4	
4	3		3	0	
5			4	0	
6			5	2	
7				–3	
8				0	
9				12	
10				8	
11					

Example 3

This flowchart inputs number of hours sunshine each day over a 7 day week. It outputs the highest value recorded and the average (mean) number of hours sunshine per day.

The following data is to be used: 8.2, 0.0, 0.0, 11.4, 6.8, 5.7, 9.9.

Flowchart

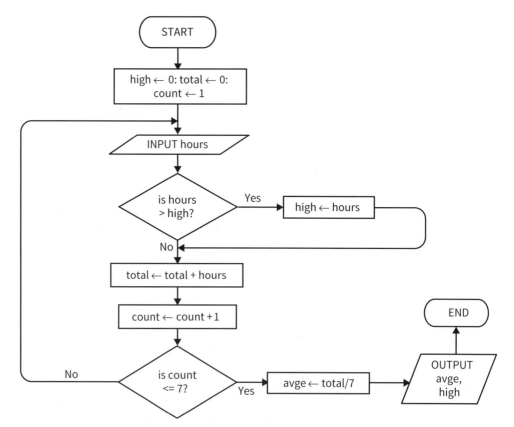

Trace table

high	count	total	hours	avge	OUTPUT
0	1	0	8.2	6.0	6.0, 11.4
8.2	2	8.2			
	3	8.2	0.0		
	4	8.2	0.0		
11.4	5	19.6	11.4		
	6	26.4	6.8		
	7	32.1	5.7		
	8	42.0	9.9		

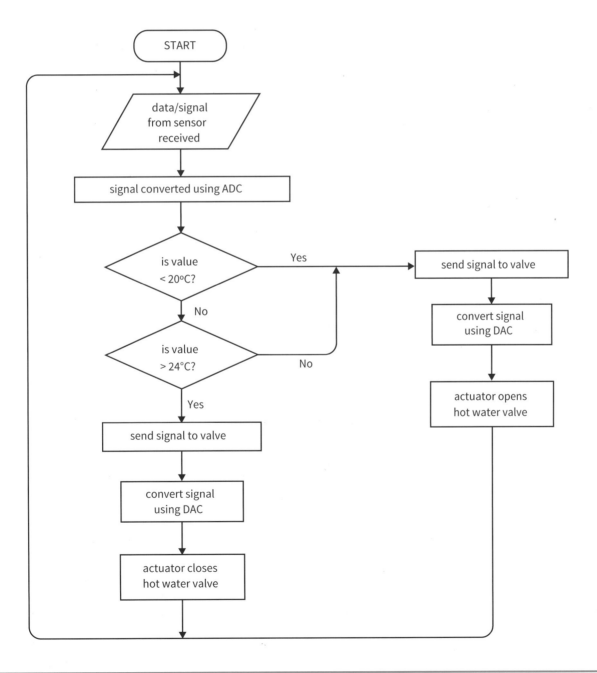

Flowcharts can also be used to represent an operation of some kind (for example, controlling the environment in a greenhouse and monitoring for intruders in a house). The following flowchart shows how a temperature sensor is being used to maintain a temperature between 20°C and 25°C by opening and closing a hot water valve.

6.5 End of chapter questions

6.5.1 Igor lives in Russia and frequently travels to Singapore (time difference: +6 hours), Western Canada (time difference: −10 hours) and India (time difference: +3.5 hours).

Write an algorithm, in the form of a flowchart, which inputs the present time (using the 24 hour clock) and the country he is visiting. The output will be the time in the country he is visiting.

Extension to question: take into account data such as time in Russia: 19:45 which means it will be 01:45 the NEXT day in Singapore, or 08:00 in Russia which means it is 22:00 the PREVIOUS day in Canada or consider the calculation problems with India due to a fractional time difference of +3.5 (for example, if it is 16:40 in Russia then it will be 20:15 in India which means BOTH the hour AND minutes need to be updated).

6.5.2 A large school categorises its students as Year 1, Year 2, up to Year 7. The school is interested in finding out how many Year 1 students are taller than 135 cm and how many Year 7 students are shorter than 175 cm.

Write an algorithm, in the form of a flowchart, which inputs the Year number and height of all 1000 students. The output will be how many students in Year 1 were taller than 135 cm and how many students in Year 7 were shorter than 175 cm.

6.5.3 A class has decided to count the number of vehicles per day passing over a bridge near their school. Readings were taken for a whole year.

Write an algorithm, in the form of a flowchart, which inputs the number of vehicles per day passing over the bridge for the whole year (you may assume that a year contains 365 days). The output will be the average (mean) number of vehicles per day and the highest number of vehicles per day during the survey.

6.5.4 A small store sells 650 items in a day. Each item sold is identified by a 3-digit code. All items which start with a 0 (zero) are sweets, all items that start with a 1 are stationery, all items that start with a 2 are books and all items that start with a 3 are drinks. Thus:

000 to 099 are sweets

100 to 199 are stationery

200 to 299 are books

300 to 399 are drinks

Write an algorithm, in the form of a flowchart, which inputs the 3-digit code for all 650 items sold and outputs what per cent were sweets, what per cent were stationery, what per cent were books and what per cent were drinks.

6.5.5 The rainfall (in mm) and number of hours sunshine are being recorded for ten (10) holiday resorts. Readings were taken every day for a whole year (365 days).

Write an algorithm, in the form of a flowchart, which:

- inputs the daily rainfall and number of hours of sunshine for EACH holiday resort over the year

- outputs the average rainfall for EACH resort over the year

- outputs the average number of hours of sunshine for EACH resort over the year

- outputs the highest number of hours sunshine in a day for ALL resorts over the year

- outputs the lowest rainfall in a day for ALL resorts over the year.

6.5.6 Traffic enforcement cameras read the time it takes a vehicle to pass 2 points in the road 500 metres apart. The speed of the vehicle is calculated using:

$$speed = \frac{30}{(time\ taken\ in\ minutes)}\ km/hour$$

The maximum speed allowed is 100 km/hour. Eight thousand (8000) vehicles were monitored using these cameras over one day.

Write an algorithm, in the form of a flowchart, which:

- inputs the time taken (in minutes) for each of the 8000 vehicles

- calculates the speed for each vehicle using the formula above

- outputs the speed of each vehicle and a message if the speed exceeds 100 km/hour

- after all the data is input, outputs how many vehicles in total exceeded the 100 km/hour speed limit; outputs the percentage of all vehicles which exceeded the speed limit

- after all the data is input, outputs the highest speed calculated.

6.5.7 A sports club charges $5 per hour per person to hire a tennis court. If there are 3 or more players, there is a 25% discount on the **total** cost per hour. A further 10% discount on the **total** cost per hour is given if they book the court for 3 hours or more. (So 4 players booking the court for 4 hours would be charged $80 – $20 – $8, i.e. $52; 5 players booking the court for 2 hours would be charged $50 – $12.50 – $0, i.e. $37.50).

Write an algorithm, in the form of a flowchart, which inputs the number of players and number of hours required and outputs the total charge for the hire of the tennis court.

Extension to question: if one of the players is a member of the club, the charge per hour drops to only $4. The player and one of the staff at the club both have to type in a 4-digit PIN to verify that the player is a club member. The 2 PINs must match if the player is to receive his $1 per hour discount.

6.5.8 Draw the trace table and determine the output for the following flowchart using the following data: 52, –20, 3.

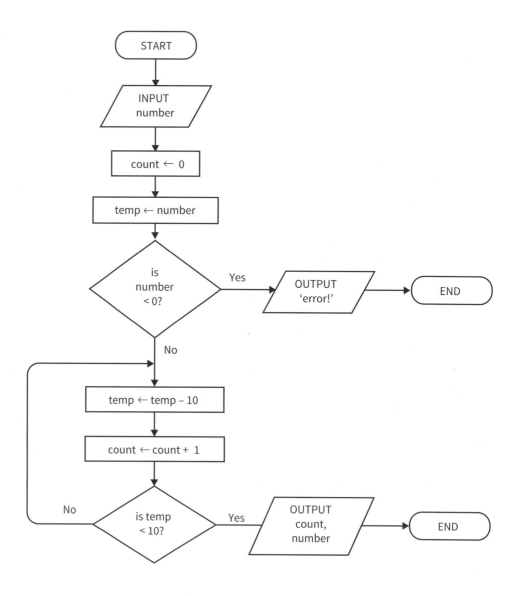

Trace table

number	count	temp	OUTPUT

6.5.9 Draw the trace table and determine the output for the following flowchart using the following data:

sunny, sunny, wet, foggy, sunny, wet, sunny, wet, foggy, sunny, last.

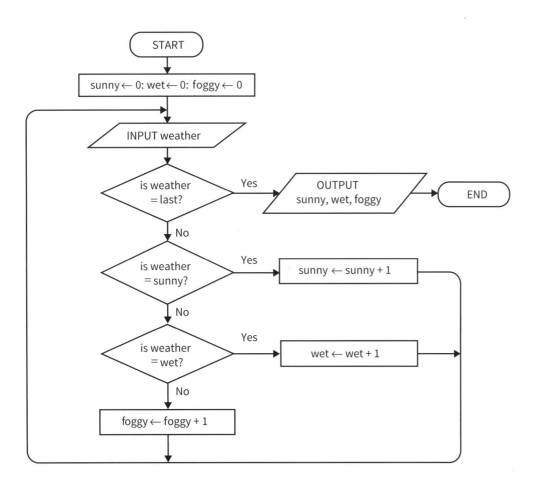

Trace table

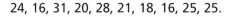

6.5.10 Draw the trace table and determine the output for the following flowchart using the following data:

24, 16, 31, 20, 28, 21, 18, 16, 25, 25.

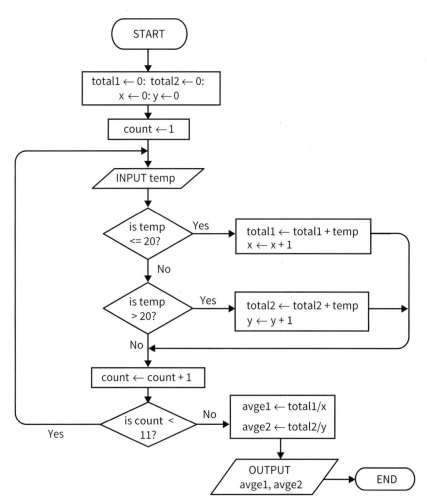

Trace table

total1	total2	x	y	count	temp	avge1	avge2	OUTPUT

6.5.11 Draw the trace table for the following flowchart using the following data:

40, −5, 3400, 800000.

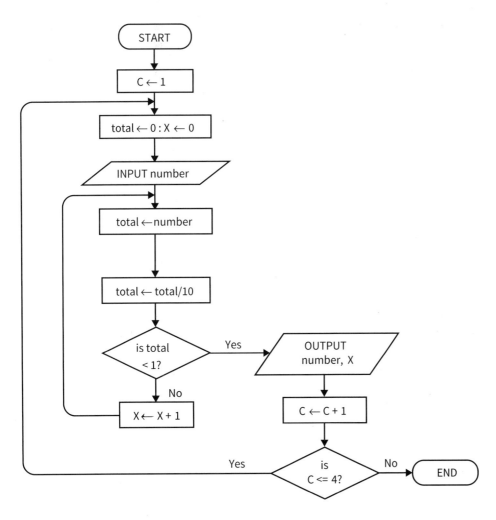

Trace table

C	total	X	number	OUTPUT

7 Pseudocode

In this chapter you will learn about:
- *Pseudocode*
- *Solving problems using pseudocode*

This chapter will look at pseudocode and show how it can be used to solve a problem.

7.1 Pseudocode

In chapter 6, you learnt how flowcharts can be used to solve problems. Another method involves the use of *pseudocode.*

Key Point — **This is not an actual programming language but is a way of representing the more common types of language constructs.**

Common pseudocode constructs

Assignment

Assignment statements are used to set a variable to a new value; for example, **start ← 1** or **percent ← value / total * 100**. The new value can be a constant or an expression.

Counting

Counting is a very common task in many programming languages; for example, **count ← count + 1** which means, in computer terms, *new count ← old count + 1* and is simply a count in 1's.

Totals

This construct adds a series of values together; for example, **total ← total + number** which means, in computer terms, *new total ← old total + number*.

Input and output

These commands input data into a computer and output data following some form of processing; for example, **input temp** (sometimes written as **read temp**) and **output sum** (sometimes written as **print sum**).

> It is possible to count in any increment required; for example, count = count + 0.5 or count = count − 1 (this is counting backwards).

If statements and case statements

These are conditional statements in that some condition must be met before the next statement is executed. The format of each statement is:

if ... then ... (else) ... (endif)
case ... of ... otherwise ... endcase

Look at the following example:

> **Note that both pieces of code do the same thing: if value = 1 then total is incremented by 20, if the value is 2 then the total is incremented by 50; any other value causes an error message.**

1. **case** value **of**

    1: total ← total + 20
    2: total ← total + 50

    otherwise print 'error'
    endcase

2. **if** value = 1
    then total ← total + 20
    else if value = 2
        then total ← total + 50
        else print 'error'

Loops

There are three common ways of carrying out a loop. All the following pieces of code carry out the same task: input 40 numbers and output their total.

The first loop is a **for... to** loop:

```
for count = 1 to 40
    input number              (or read number)
    total ← total + number
next count
output total                  (or print total)
```

The next loop is a **while ... do ... endwhile** loop:

```
count = 1
while count < 41 do           (or while count <= 40)
    input number
    count ← count + 1
endwhile
output total
```

The next loop is a **repeat ... until** loop:

```
count = 1
repeat
    input number
    count ← count + 1
until count > 40
output total
```

It is possible to set the count to 0 instead of 1 at the start of the while or repeat loop; this would mean using *while count < 40* and *until count > 39* or *until count = 40*.

7.2   Solving problems using pseudocode

The following problems can all be solved using pseudocode. Each follows a logical series of steps; but no single correct solution exists, and the following are simply guidelines on good pseudocode construction.

Problem 1

A garage sells cars. The amount of road tax is based on engine size. Engines over 3 litres in size incur a tax of $500, engines over 2 litres in size incur a tax of $300 and engines over 1 litre in size are taxed at the rate of $100. Cars with engines below 1 litre incur no road tax. Write an algorithm, using pseudocode, to show the tax due on any car sold by the garage.

Solution

```
input engine
if engine > 3 then tax ← 500
   else if engine > 2 then tax ← 300
      else if engine > 1 then tax ← 100
         else tax ← 0
output tax
```

Problem 2

The heights of 500 students in a school are being measured. Write an algorithm, using pseudocode, which inputs all 500 heights and outputs how many students were taller than 1.45 metres or shorter than 1.45 metres.

Solution

```
total1 ← 0: total2 ← 0
   for count ← 1 to 500
      input height
      if height > 1.45 then total1 ← total1 + 1
      if height < 1.45 then total2 ← total2 + 1
   next count
   output total1, total2
```

Notice that the use of the **else** part of the **if** statement is not required here since the two **if** statements are not connected, unlike in example 1 where each step was conditional on the result of the previous step; it would be equally correct to use the **while … do … endwhile** and **repeat … until** statements in this answer.

Problem 3

Write an algorithm, using pseudocode, which:
– inputs the weight of 1000 items
– outputs the weight of the heaviest and the lightest item
– outputs the average (mean) weight of all the items input.

Solution

```
heaviest ← 0: lightest ← 100: total ← 0
for count ← 1 to 1000
    input weight
    if weight > heaviest then heaviest ← weight
        else if weight < lightest then lightest ← weight
    total ← total + weight
next count
average ← total/1000
output average, heaviest, lightest
```

In the first line, it was necessary to set lightest to a value which was unlikely to be encountered – if it was set at 0, the value lightest = 0 would have been retained throughout the program since none of the input weights would have been smaller than 0; hence the lightest weight would probably be missed altogether; in the fourth line, a check is made to see if the new weight is greater than the existing value stored in heaviest – if the new value is larger, then heaviest takes this new value; the argument in the fifth line is similar except this time we're looking for smaller values being input.

Problem 4

A small shop sells sweets, magazines and drinks. Each item sold is identified by a unique 4-digit code. All sweets sold have a code that starts with a 1, all magazines sold have a code that starts with a 2 and all drinks sold have a code that starts with a 3. So:

1000 to 1999 are the codes for sweets,
2000 to 2999 are the codes for magazines, and
3000 to 3999 are the codes for drinks.
(9999 is used to stop the algorithm)

Write an algorithm, using pseudocode, which inputs the codes for all of the items sold in the shop and outputs how many items sold were sweets, magazines or drinks.

Solution

```
sweets ← 0: mags ← 0: drinks ← 0
input code
while code ≠ 9999 do
    number ← 0
        repeat
            code ← code – 1000
            if code >= 0 then number ← number + 1
        until code < 0
    case number of
        1: sweets ← sweets + 1
        2: mags ← mags + 1
```

It is also possible to replace lines 9 to 14 with *if … then … else* statements:

```
if number = 1 then sweets
                ← sweets + 1
    else if = 2 then mags
        number ← mags + 1
```

>   3: drinks ← drinks + 1
>   **otherwise print** 'error – wrong code'
>   **endcase**
>   **input** code
>   **endwhile**
>   **output** sweets, mags, drinks

>   ***else if*** *number = 3*
>   ***then*** *drinks + 1*
>   ***else output*** *'error –*
>   *wrong code'*

In the second line the first code is input outside the loop to allow the program to deal with all data items – if 9999 is the first data item, then an error message would be produced as the program tries to process the data – this method allows an outer loop to be used to control the inputs and also stops the program as soon as 9999 is input; the **input** code in the end is used to input the next code which is now inside the ***while ... do ... endwhile*** loop; note that a ***for ... to*** loop could not be used since we do not know how many data items need to be input.

> **9999 is in fact used to stop the program and allow output.**

Problem 5

Some students have been carrying out 5 experiments; 20 temperature readings were taken in each experiment.

Write an algorithm, using pseudocode, which inputs all of the temperature readings, and outputs the average (mean) temperature for each experiment, the average (mean) temperature for all 20 experiments and the highest temperature recorded from all the readings taken.

Solution

>   highest ← –100: total_all ← 0
>   **for** expt ← 1 **to** 5
>   total_expt ← 0
>   **for** reading ← 1 **to** 20
>   **input** temp
>   total_expt ← total_expt + temp
>   total_all ← total_all + temp
>   **if** temp > highest **then** highest ← temp
>   **next** reading
>   average_expt ← total_expt/20
>   **output** average_expt
>   **next** expt
>   average_all ← total_all/100
>   **output** average_all

Notice that this problem uses ***nested loops***, i.e. one loop inside another loop; the outer loop (expt) controls the number of experiments whereas the inner loop (reading) controls the number of readings per experiment; in the third line, total_expt has to be set to 0 each time before entering the reading loop.

7.3 End of chapter questions

Questions 7.3.1 to 7.3.3 contain sections of pseudocode which contain errors. Locate these errors and suggest a correction.

7.3.1 The following section of pseudocode inputs 5000 numbers and outputs the largest positive number and the largest negative number (i.e. MOST negative number). There are four errors in total.

```
1 input number
2 neg ← number: pos ← number
3 for x ← 1 to 5000
4    input number
5    if number > pos then number ← pos
6    if number < neg then number ← neg
7    x ← x + 1
8 next x
9 output pos, neg
```

7.3.2 The following section of pseudocode inputs the number of people buying some tickets at $5 each. A 10 per cent discount is given if three or more tickets are bought. The printed tickets are output. There are three errors in total.

```
1 input no_ppl
2 cost ← no_ppl * 5
3 if no_ppl > 4 then cost ← cost * 0.10
4 for x ← 0 to no_ppl
5    print ticket
6 next x
```

7.3.3 The following section of pseudocode inputs 100 numbers and outputs how many numbers were 1000 or over and how many were under 1000. There are five errors in total.

```
1 count ← 0
2 total_one ← 1: total_two ← 1
3 while count <= 100 do
4    if number > 1000 then total_one ← total_one + 1
5    if number < 1000 then total_two ←= total_two + 1
6    input number
7    c ← c + 1
8 endwhile
9 output total_one, total_two
```

Questions 7.3.4 to 7.3.10 are problems which require an algorithm to be written in pseudocode.

7.3.4 Igor lives in Russia and frequently travels to Singapore (time difference: +6 hours), Western Canada (time difference: –10 hours) and India (time difference: +3.5 hours).

Write an algorithm, using pseudocode only, which inputs the present time (using the 24 hour clock) and the country he is visiting. The output will be the time in the country he is visiting.

(Extension to question: take into account data such as time in Russia: 19:45 which means it will be 01:45 the NEXT day in Singapore, or 08:00 in Russia which means it is 22:00 the PREVIOUS day in Canada or consider the calculation problems with India due to a fractional time difference of +3.5; for example, if it is 16:40 in Russia then it will be 20:15 in India which means BOTH the hour AND minutes need to be updated).

7.3.5 A large school categorises its students as Year 1, Year 2, up to Year 7. The school is interested in finding out how many Year 1 students are taller than 135 cm and how many Year 7 students are shorter than 175 cm.

Write an algorithm, using pseudocode only, which inputs the Year number and height of all 1000 students. The output will be how many students in Year 1 were taller than 135 cm and how many students in Year 7 were shorter than 175 cm.

7.3.6 A class has decided to count the number of vehicles per day passing over a bridge near their school. Readings were taken for a whole year.

Write an algorithm, using pseudocode only, which inputs the number of vehicles per day passing over the bridge for the whole year (you may assume that a year contains 365 days). The output will be the average (mean) number of vehicles per day and the highest number of vehicles per day during the survey.

7.3.7 A small store sells 650 items in a day. Each item sold is identified by a 3-digit code. All items which start with a 0 (zero) are sweets, all items that start with a 1 are stationery, all items that start with a 2 are books and all items that start with a 3 are drinks. Thus:

000 to 099 are sweets

100 to 199 are stationery

200 to 299 are books

300 to 399 are drinks

Write an algorithm, using pseudocode only, which inputs the 3-digit code for all 650 items sold and outputs what per cent were sweets, what per cent were stationery, what per cent were books and what per cent were drinks.

7.3.8 The rainfall (in mm) and number of hours sunshine are being recorded for ten (10) holiday resorts. Readings were taken every day for a whole year (365 days).

Write an algorithm, using pseudocode only, which:

- inputs the daily rainfall and number of hours of sunshine for EACH holiday resort over the year
- outputs the average rainfall for EACH resort over the year
- outputs the average number of hours of sunshine for EACH resort over the year
- outputs the highest number of hours sunshine in a day for ALL resorts over the year
- outputs the lowest rainfall in a day for ALL resorts over the year.

7.3.9 Traffic enforcement cameras read the time it takes a vehicle to pass 2 points in the road 500 metres apart. The speed of the vehicle is calculated using:

$$\text{speed} = \frac{30}{\text{(time taken in minutes)}} \text{ km/hour}$$

The maximum speed allowed is 100 km/hour. Eight thousand (8000) vehicles were monitored using these cameras over one day.

Write an algorithm, using pseudocode only, which:

- inputs the time taken (in minutes) for each of the 8000 vehicles
- calculates the speed for each vehicle using the formula above
- outputs the speed of each vehicle AND a message if the speed exceeds 100 km/hour
- after all the data is input, outputs how many vehicles in total exceeded the 100 km/hour speed limit; outputs the percentage of all vehicles which exceeded the speed limit
- after all the data is input, outputs the highest speed calculated.

7.3.10 A sports club charges $5 per hour per person to hire a tennis court. If there are 3 or more players, there is a 25 per cent discount on the **total** cost per hour. A further 10 per cent discount on the **total** cost per hour is given if they book the court for 3 hours or more. So 4 players booking the court for 4 hours would be charged $80 – $20 – $8, i.e. $52; 5 players booking the court for 2 hours would be charged $50 – $12.50 – $0, i.e. $37.50.

Write an algorithm, using pseudocode only, which inputs the number of players and number of hours required and outputs the total charge for the hire of the tennis court.

(Extension to question: If one of the players is a member of the club, the charge per hour drops to only $4. The player and one of the staff at the club both have to type in a 4-digit PIN to verify that the player is a club member. The 2 PINs must match if the player is to receive his $1 per hour discount.)

8 Logic gates

Learning Summary

In this chapter you will learn about:
- *Logic gates*
- *Truth tables*
- *Logic circuits/networks*

In this chapter we will look at how logic gates are used and how truth tables are used to check if combinations of logic gates (known as logic circuits or logic networks) carry out the required functions.

8.1 Logic gates

A large number of electronic circuits (in computers, control units and so on) are made up of logic gates. These process signals which represent true or false.

> Signals can be represented as ON or OFF, 1 or 0 as well.

The most common symbols used to represent logic gates are shown below. In this book, we will use the **MIL symbols**. But the reader may also see the simpler, more general, logic gate representations.

NOT   AND   OR   NAND   NOR   XOR

MIL symbols

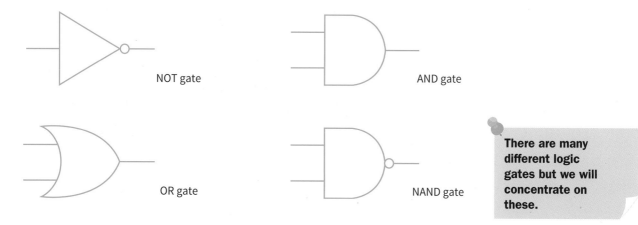

NOT gate   AND gate

OR gate   NAND gate

> There are many different logic gates but we will concentrate on these.

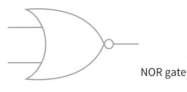
NOR gate

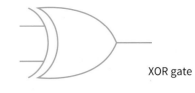
XOR gate

8.2 Truth tables

Truth tables are used to show logic gate functions. The NOT gate has only one input, but all the others have two inputs.

When constructing a truth table, the binary values 1 and 0 are used. Every possible combination, depending on number of inputs, is produced. Basically, the number of possible combinations of 1s and 0s is 2^n where n = number of inputs. For example, 2 inputs have 2^2 combinations (i.e. 4), 3 inputs have 2^3 combinations (i.e. 8) and so on. The next section shows how these truth tables are used.

Description of the six logic gates

NOT gate

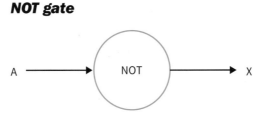

The output (X) is **true** (i.e. 1 or ON) if:

INPUT A is **NOT TRUE** (i.e. 0 or OFF)

Truth table for: **X = NOT A**

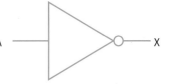

INPUT A	OUTPUT X
0	1
1	0

AND gate

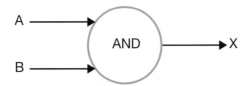

The output (X) is **true** (i.e. 1 or ON) if:

INPUT A AND INPUT B are **BOTH TRUE** (i.e. 1 or ON)

Truth table for: **X = A AND B**

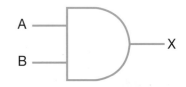

INPUT A	INPUT B	OUTPUT X
0	0	0
0	1	0
1	0	0
1	1	1

OR gate

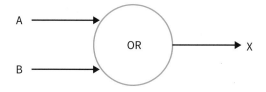

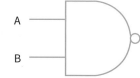

INPUT A	INPUT B	OUTPUT X
0	0	0
0	1	1
1	0	1
1	1	1

The output (X) is **true** (i.e. 1 or ON) if:

INPUT A OR INPUT B is TRUE (i.e. 1 or ON)

Truth table for: *X = A OR B*

NAND gate

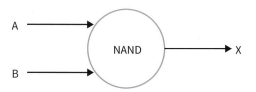

INPUT A	INPUT B	OUTPUT X
0	0	1
0	1	1
1	0	1
1	1	0

The output (X) is **true** (i.e. 1 or ON) if:

INPUT A AND INPUT B are **NOT BOTH TRUE** (i.e. 1 or ON)

Truth table for: **X = NOT (A AND B)**

NOR gate

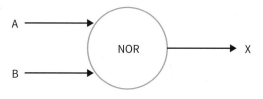

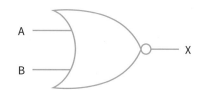

INPUT A	INPUT B	OUTPUT X
0	0	1
0	1	0
1	0	0
1	1	0

The output (X) is **true** (i.e. 1 or ON) if:

INPUT A OR INPUT B are **NOT BOTH TRUE** (i.e. 1 or ON)

Truth table for: **X = NOT (A OR B)**

XOR gate

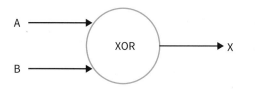

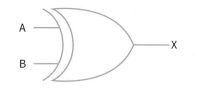

The output (X) is **true** (i.e. 1 or ON) if:

(INPUT A AND (NOT INPUT B)) OR
((NOT INPUT A) AND INPUT B)
is **TRUE** (i.e. 1 or ON)

(i.e. one of the inputs is 1 but not both)
Truth table for: **X = (A AND (NOT B)) OR**
((NOT A) AND B)

INPUT A	INPUT B	OUTPUT X
0	0	0
0	1	1
1	0	1
1	1	0

All of the above logic statements can be replaced by algebraic statements
(i.e. *Boolean expressions*). Whilst this is outside the scope of this text book,
readers may wish to investigate Boolean algebra further.

logic gate	Boolean expression
NOT A	$\bar{A}$
A AND B	$A . B$
A OR B	$A + B$
A NAND B	$\overline{A . B}$
A NOR B	$(\overline{A + B})$
A XOR B	$(A . \bar{B}) + (\bar{A} . B)$

8.3   Logic circuits/networks

Logic gates can be combined together to produce more complex logic
circuits (networks).

> **Key Point** **The output from a logic circuit (network) is checked by
> producing a truth table.**

Two different types of problem are considered here:

– drawing the truth table from a given logic circuit (network)
– designing a logic circuit (network) from a given problem and testing it
  by also drawing a truth table.

Example 1

Produce a truth table from the following logic circuit (network).

First part

There are three inputs; thus we must have 2^3 (i.e. 8) possible combinations
of 1s and 0s.

To find the values (outputs) at points **P** and **Q**, it is necessary to consider the
truth tables for the NOR gate (output P) and the AND gate (output Q), i.e.

P = A **NOR** B
Q = B **AND** C

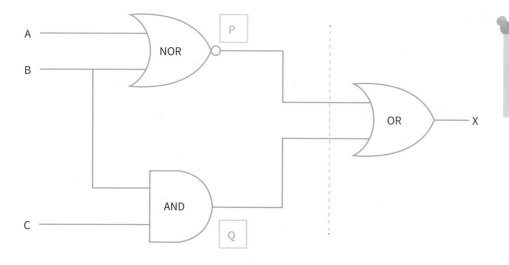

To show how this works, we will split the logic circuit into two parts (shown by the dotted line).

We thus get:

INPUT A	INPUT B	INPUT C	OUTPUT P	OUTPUT Q
0	0	0	1	0
0	0	1	1	0
0	1	0	0	0
0	1	1	0	1
1	0	0	0	0
1	0	1	0	0
1	1	0	0	0
1	1	1	0	1

Second part

There are eight values from **P** and **Q** which form the inputs to the last **OR** gate.

Hence we get X = P **OR** Q which gives the following truth table:

INPUT P	INPUT Q	OUTPUT X
1	0	1
1	0	1
0	0	0
0	1	1
0	0	0
0	0	0
0	0	0
0	1	1

Which now gives us the final truth table for the logic circuit given at the start of the example:

INPUT A	INPUT B	INPUT C	OUTPUT X
0	0	0	1
0	0	1	1
0	1	0	0
0	1	1	1
1	0	0	0
1	0	1	0
1	1	0	0
1	1	1	1

Example 2

Consider the following problem.

A system used three switches A, B and C; a combination of switches determines whether an alarm, X, sounds:

If switch A or switch B are in the ON position and if switch C is in the OFF position then a signal to sound an alarm, X is produced.

> Remembering that ON = 1 and OFF = 0; also remember that we write 0 as NOT 1.

It is possible to convert this problem into a logic statement.

So we get:

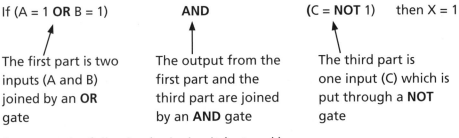

If (A = 1 **OR** B = 1)   **AND**   (C = **NOT** 1)   then X = 1

The first part is two inputs (A and B) joined by an **OR** gate

The output from the first part and the third part are joined by an **AND** gate

The third part is one input (C) which is put through a **NOT** gate

So we get the following logic circuit (network):

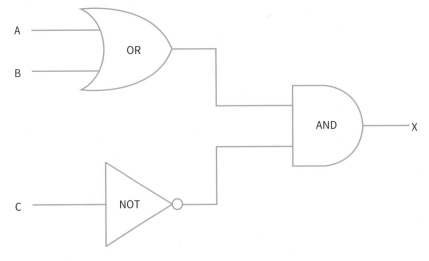

This gives the following truth table:

INPUT A	INPUT B	INPUT C	OUTPUT X
0	0	0	0
0	0	1	0
0	1	0	1
0	1	1	0
1	0	0	1
1	0	1	0
1	1	0	1
1	1	1	0

Example 3

A manufacturing process is controlled by a built in logic circuit which is made up of AND, OR and NOT gates only. The process receives a STOP signal (i.e. X = 1) depending on certain conditions, shown in the following table.

INPUTS	BINARY VALUES	CONDITION IN PROCESS
V	1	Volume > 1000 litres
	0	Volume <= 1000 litres
T	1	Temperature > 750°C
	0	Temperature <= 750°C
S	1	Speed > 15 metres/second (m/s)
	0	Speed <= 15 metres/ second (m/s)

A stop signal (X = 1) occurs when:

either   Volume, V > 1000 litres and Speed, S <= 15 m/s

or   Temperature, T <= 750°C and Speed, S > 15 m/s

Draw the logic circuit and truth table to show all the possible situations when the stop signal could be received.

First of all, it is necessary to turn the problem into a series of logic statements:

- statement 1 can now be re-written as:
  V = 1 **AND** S = **NOT** 1 since V > 1000 (binary value = 1) and S <= 15 (binary value = 0)
- statement 2 can now be re-written as:
  T = **NOT** 1 **AND** S = 1 since T <= 750°C (binary value = 0) and S > 15 (binary value = 1)
- both statements are joined together by an **OR gate**.

So, our logic statement becomes:
X = 1 if (V = 1 **AND** S = **NOT** 1) **OR** (T = **NOT** 1 **AND** S = 1)

We can now draw the logic circuit (network) by constructing it for statement 1 and for statement 2 and joining them with an **OR** gate.

In the following logic circuit note that V has been placed at the bottom of logic diagram – this is done to avoid crossing over of lines which makes it look neater and less complex. It is not essential to do this and is only done for the reasons given.

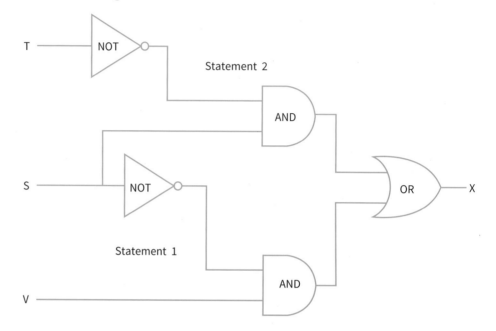

We can now construct the truth table:

INPUT V	INPUT T	INPUT S	OUTPUT X
0	0	0	0
0	0	1	1
0	1	0	0
0	1	1	0
1	0	0	1
1	0	1	1
1	1	0	1
1	1	1	0

8.4 End of chapter questions

In questions 8.4.1 to 8.4.6 produce truth tables from the given logic circuits (networks). Remember, if there are two inputs then there will be four possible outputs; if there are three inputs then there will be eight possible outputs. The truth tables will look like this:

INPUT A	INPUT B	OUTPUT X
0	0	
0	1	
1	0	
1	1	

INPUT A	INPUT B	INPUT C	OUTPUT X
0	0	0	
0	0	1	
0	1	0	
0	1	1	
1	0	0	
1	0	1	
1	1	0	
1	1	1	

8.4.1

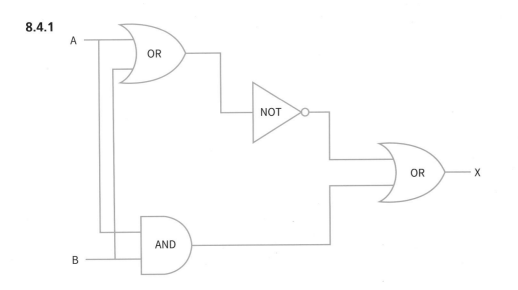

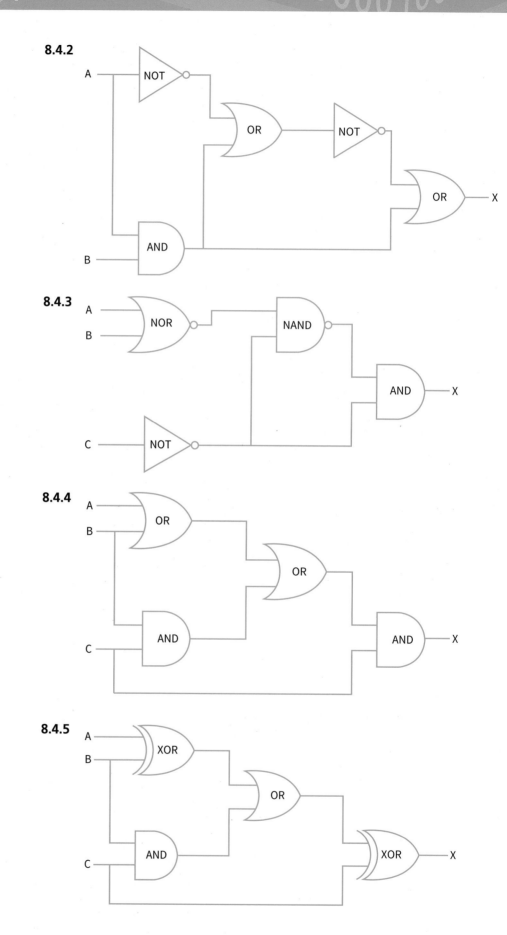

8.4.2

8.4.3

8.4.4

8.4.5

8.4.6

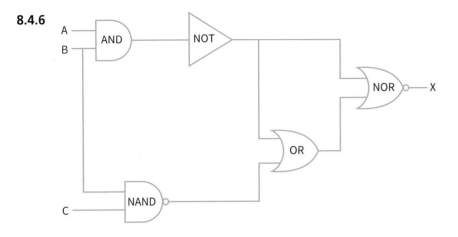

Questions 8.4.7 to 8.4.10 require both the logic circuit (network) and the truth table to be drawn. The truth table can be derived from the logic circuit (network), but can also be derived from the original problem. This could therefore be used as a cross-check that the logic circuit (network) is a correct representation of the original problem.

8.4.7 An electronic system will only operate if three switches P, S and T are correctly set. An output signal (X = 1) will occur if R and S are both in the ON position **or** if R is in the OFF position and S and T are both in the ON position.

Design a logic circuit (network) to represent the above situation and also draw the truth table.

8.4.8 A traffic light system uses logic gates as part of the control system. The system is operated when the output D has the value 1. This happens when:

either   (a) signal A is red

or   (b) signal A is green and signals B and C are both red

(NOTE: You may assume for this problem that red = 0 and green = 1.)

Design a logic circuit (network) and draw the truth table for the above system.

8.4.9 A chemical process gives out a warning signal (W = 1) when the process operates incorrectly. A logic circuit (network) is used to monitor the process and to determine whether W = 1.

Inputs	Binary values	Description of plant status
C	1	Chemical rate = 20 litres/second
	0	Chemical rate < 20 litres/second
T	1	Temperature = 91°C
	0	Temperature > 91°C
X	1	Concentration > 5M
	0	Concentration = 5M

A warning signal (W = 1) will be generated if:

either (a) Chemical rate < 20 litres/second

or (b) Temperature > 91°C and Concentration > 5M

or (c) Chemical rate = 20 litres/second and Temperature > 91°C

Draw a logic circuit (network) and truth table to show all the possible situations when the warning signal could be received.

8.4.10 A nuclear power station has a safety system based on three inputs to a logic circuit (network). A warning signal (S = 1) is produced when certain conditions in the nuclear power station occur based on these three inputs.

Inputs	Binary values	Description of plant status
T	1	Temperature > 115°C
	0	Temperature <= 115°C
P	1	Reactor pressure > 15 bar
	0	Reactor pressure <= 15 bar
W	1	Cooling water > 120 litres/hour
	0	Cooling water <= 120 litres/hour

A warning signal (S = 1) will be produced when any of the following occurs:

either (a) Temperature > 115°C and Cooling water <= 120 litres/hour

or (b) Temperature <= 115°C and Reactor pressure > 15 bar or Cooling water <= 120 litres/hour

Draw a logic circuit (network) and truth table to show all the possible situations when the warning signal (S) could be received.

Chapter

9 Computer ethics

Learning Summary

In this chapter you will learn about:

- *Computer ethics*
- *Free software*
- *Freeware*
- *Shareware*

There are many varieties of software available in the market; without good software, computer systems would have had far less impact on society as a whole.

This chapter will consider a number of common software applications and its key attributes.

9.1 Computer ethics

Computer ethics is a set of principles that regulates the use of computers in everyday life (both commercial and non-commercial).

This basically covers:

- intellectual property rights (for example, is it wrong to copy software without permission?)
- privacy issues (for example, accessing somebody's personal information)
- effect of computers on society

As computers continue to increase in their use in everyday life, ethical standards in their use will continue to evolve and be subject to more and more legislation to protect the individual and to protect the producers of software and associated data.

Copyright is the ownership of intellectual property. The Internet is fast becoming one of the main areas where copyright issues are becoming a major problem. Many users of the Internet believe that freedom of information also means that posting or copying any information is exempt from copyright. Nothing could be further from the truth. But just as serious, as more and more people are turning to the Internet to do research, is the problem of *plagiarism*.

Basically, plagiarism is to take somebody's ideas (whether written or verbal) and claim that these ideas are your own! The last part of this sentence is the key issue here. It is perfectly acceptable to quote another person's ideas and use these ideas to formulate your own opinions and conclusions; but some form of acknowledgement must be made to indicate that these ideas were not originally your own. These can take the form of references at the end of a document or numbered references on each page (for example, plagiarism[21]) with a note at the bottom of the page indicating the source of the material.

> Universities and colleges often use this software to check if student project work is subject to unacceptable plagiarism!

It is of course possible to re-write the ideas in your own words (changing the terminology or adapting the ideas using your own words) – this goes some way to removing the risk of plagiarism. There is also software available which can pick up work which has been taken from the Internet.

9.2 Free software, freeware and shareware

Free software

Free software is where users have the freedom to run, copy, change and adapt available software. The main concept here is one of **liberty and not price**, since free software guarantees the freedom and rights to study and modify software by having access to the source code itself. Basically, the user controls the program and what it does and has the freedom to:

- run the software for any purpose they choose
- study how the software works and change it to meet their own needs
- redistribute copies of the software to friends, family or colleagues as they see fit
- distribute modified versions/copies of the software.

There is no need to pay or ask permission to do any of the above since the software has no copyright restrictions. Free software can be commercial or non-commercial in nature. But the original software or modified versions of it must not contain coding from software which does not fall into this category since the perpetrator would then fall foul of copyright laws!

Freeware

Freeware refers to software that anyone can download for free from the Internet and then use without having to pay any fees (for example, *Adobe PDF* or *Skype*). The usual copyright laws apply to freeware and the user license is an important part of this. Unlike free software, it is not possible to modify freeware or view the source code.

Shareware

Shareware gives users the chance to try out the software free of charge before buying it (for example, *Winzip*). Clearly it is subject to all the usual copyright laws. However, all the features of the full version of the software

are not made available and the user has to buy the full version if they intend to use the software in the future. Usually the copyright holder needs to be contacted before copies of the software can be distributed to other people.

9.3 End of chapter questions

9.3.1 **(a)** Describe the main differences between free software and freeware.

(b) Explain how computer ethics could affect a user when downloading and running either freeware or shareware.

(c) A software manufacturer offers a suite of shareware programs containing a spreadsheet, computer-aided design and a word processor. Describe the main advantages and disadvantages to a user of making use of this suite of programs.

9.3.2 Explain the main differences between free software, freeware and shareware.

10 Data systems

Learning Summary

In this chapter you will learn about:
- **Data capture techniques**
- **Validation techniques**
- **Verification techniques**
- **Binary systems**
- **Hexadecimal systems**

This chapter will consider ways of capturing data both automatic and manual and will also consider how data input into a computer is checked to see if it is correct or reasonable for the application. Since computers work in binary, we will also consider binary and binary-related systems such as hexadecimal (base 16).

10.1 Data capture techniques

Data capture can be automatic or manual.

Manual data capture

Manual methods of inputting data into a computer include:

- use of keyboards/keypads wherein the user manually types in data
- touch screens where the user touches the screen to enter the data manually.

The problems associated with manual input are the relative slowness of data entry and the fact that it's error-prone.

Automatic data entry is much faster, almost error-free and usually requires little or no human intervention.

Automatic data capture

There are many ways of capturing data automatically and the method chosen is dependent on the application. Some of the more common techniques are described here.

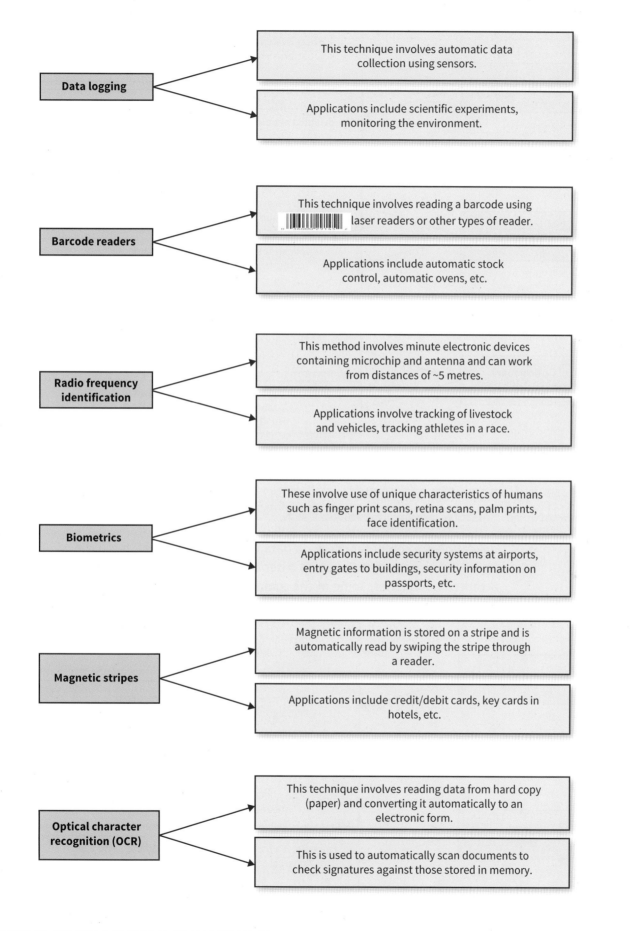

Data logging
- This technique involves automatic data collection using sensors.
- Applications include scientific experiments, monitoring the environment.

Barcode readers
- This technique involves reading a barcode using laser readers or other types of reader.
- Applications include automatic stock control, automatic ovens, etc.

Radio frequency identification
- This method involves minute electronic devices containing microchip and antenna and can work from distances of ~5 metres.
- Applications involve tracking of livestock and vehicles, tracking athletes in a race.

Biometrics
- These involve use of unique characteristics of humans such as finger print scans, retina scans, palm prints, face identification.
- Applications include security systems at airports, entry gates to buildings, security information on passports, etc.

Magnetic stripes
- Magnetic information is stored on a stripe and is automatically read by swiping the stripe through a reader.
- Applications include credit/debit cards, key cards in hotels, etc.

Optical character recognition (OCR)
- This technique involves reading data from hard copy (paper) and converting it automatically to an electronic form.
- This is used to automatically scan documents to check signatures against those stored in memory.

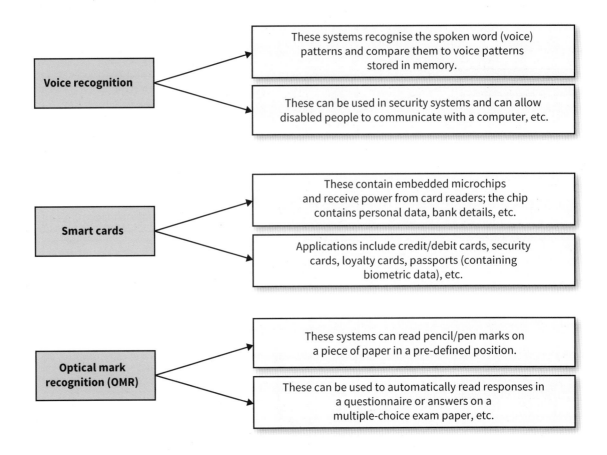

Voice recognition
- These systems recognise the spoken word (voice) patterns and compare them to voice patterns stored in memory.
- These can be used in security systems and can allow disabled people to communicate with a computer, etc.

Smart cards
- These contain embedded microchips and receive power from card readers; the chip contains personal data, bank details, etc.
- Applications include credit/debit cards, security cards, loyalty cards, passports (containing biometric data), etc.

Optical mark recognition (OMR)
- These systems can read pencil/pen marks on a piece of paper in a pre-defined position.
- These can be used to automatically read responses in a questionnaire or answers on a multiple-choice exam paper, etc.

10.2 Validation techniques

Validation is a computer check on data which is being input. It is a check to see if the data satisfies certain criteria and is reasonable, i.e. falls with accepted boundaries. Some of the common uses are described below.

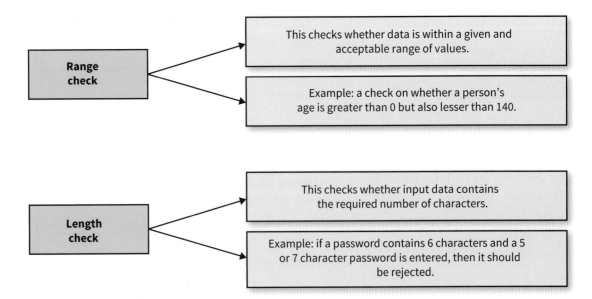

Range check
- This checks whether data is within a given and acceptable range of values.
- Example: a check on whether a person's age is greater than 0 but also lesser than 140.

Length check
- This checks whether input data contains the required number of characters.
- Example: if a password contains 6 characters and a 5 or 7 character password is entered, then it should be rejected.

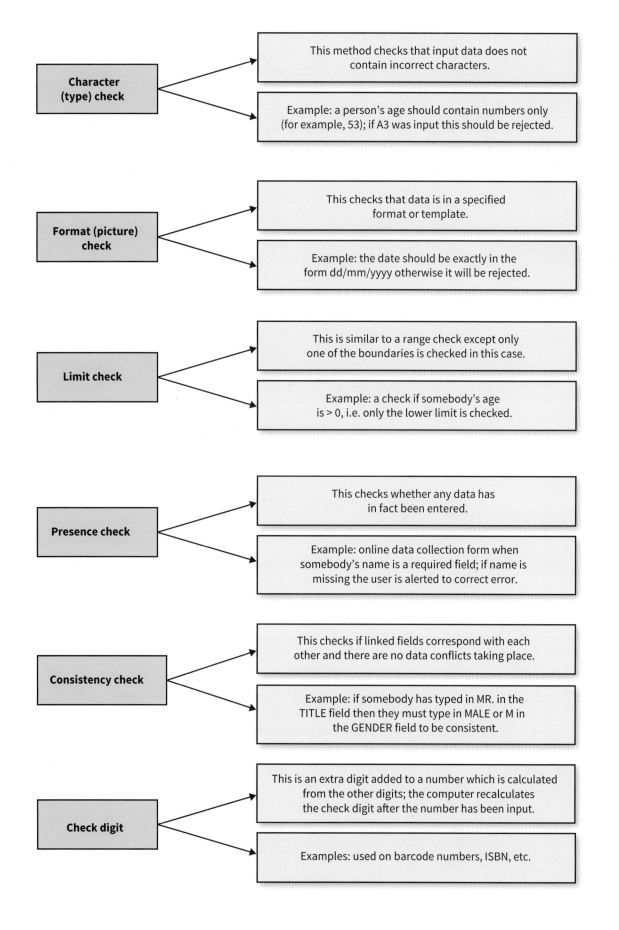

Character (type) check

This method checks that input data does not contain incorrect characters.

Example: a person's age should contain numbers only (for example, 53); if A3 was input this should be rejected.

Format (picture) check

This checks that data is in a specified format or template.

Example: the date should be exactly in the form dd/mm/yyyy otherwise it will be rejected.

Limit check

This is similar to a range check except only one of the boundaries is checked in this case.

Example: a check if somebody's age is > 0, i.e. only the lower limit is checked.

Presence check

This checks whether any data has in fact been entered.

Example: online data collection form when somebody's name is a required field; if name is missing the user is alerted to correct error.

Consistency check

This checks if linked fields correspond with each other and there are no data conflicts taking place.

Example: if somebody has typed in MR. in the TITLE field then they must type in MALE or M in the GENDER field to be consistent.

Check digit

This is an extra digit added to a number which is calculated from the other digits; the computer recalculates the check digit after the number has been input.

Examples: used on barcode numbers, ISBN, etc.

Let's take a more detailed look at the check digit system. There are a number of ways that check digits are generated; in the example that follows, we will consider the *ISBN-10 method* which makes use of the *modulo 11 system*.

> **Key Point**
> **In this method, the numbers 0 to 9 and the letter 'X' (equal to 10) can be check digits.**

Example 1

> **Here '?' is the missing check digit.**

We will consider the number 0 – 221 – 43256 – ?

(i) The position of each digit is first considered:

10	9	8	7	6	5	4	3	2	1	←	digit position
0	2	2	1	4	3	2	5	6	?	←	number

(ii) Each digit in the number is then multiplied by its digit position and the totals added together:

i.e. $(0 \times 10) + (2 \times 9) + (2 \times 8) + (1 \times 7) + (4 \times 6) + (3 \times 5) + (2 \times 4) + (5 \times 3) + (6 \times 2)$

$= 0 + 18 + 16 + 7 + 24 + 15 + 8 + 15 + 12$

$= 115$ (total)

(iii) The total is then divided by 11 (modulo 11) and the remainder, if any, is subtracted from 11. The answer then gives the *check digit*.

i.e. $115 / 11 = 10$ remainder **5**

i.e. $11 - 5 = 6$ (check digit)

hence, the final number is: **0 – 221 – 43256 – 6**

Example 2

This example shows how the check digit is re-calculated. To check the correctness of the check digit, the computer re-calculates it as follows. Suppose the following number has been input (using ISBN-10 method to calculate check digit):

0 – 444 – 39172 – X

(i) The position of each digit is first considered:

10	9	8	7	6	5	4	3	2	1	←	digit position
0	4	4	4	3	9	1	7	2	X	←	number

(ii) Each digit in the number is then multiplied by its digit position and the totals added together:

> **Always remember that X = 10.**

i.e. $(0 \times 10) + (4 \times 9) + (4 \times 8) + (4 \times 7) + (3 \times 6) + (9 \times 5) + (1 \times 4) + (7 \times 3) + (2 \times 2) + (10 \times 1)$

$= 0 + 36 + 32 + 28 + 18 + 45 + 4 + 21 + 4 + 10$

$= 198$ (total)

(iii) The total is then divided by 11; if there is NO remainder then the check digit is correct:

i.e. $198 / 11 = 18$ remainder **0**

hence, the check digit was correct.

Note that check digits can essentially identify three types of error:

- if two digits have been inverted:
  for example, 23496 instead of 23946.
- if an incorrect digit has been input:
  for example, 23996 instead of 23946.
- if a digit has been omitted or an extra digit added:
  for example, 2396 or 239966 instead of 23946.

10.3   Verification techniques

Verification is a way of preventing errors when data is copied from one medium to another. There are a number of methods used to do this which are either manual or computer-based.

Do not confuse verification with *proof reading* where no second medium is involved – only the paper document or on screen document are checked but not against each other; with proof reading only one medium is read to see if it makes sense or there are no spelling mistakes.

> This is useful when data is being copied from hard copy to computer file on a CD.

Double entry

Here data is entered *twice* (by two different people) and the computer checks that they match up; an error message is output if there are any discrepancies.

Visual check

As the name suggests, this is a manual system; the original data is compared to data typed in by manually reading it and checking against the original document.

Parity check

This is a technique used to check whether or not data has been corrupted following data transmission or copying of data from one medium to another. A group of bits is allocated a *parity bit* which is added onto the end before transmission takes place. Systems that use *even parity* require an even number of 1s in each group of bits; systems that use *odd parity* require an odd number of 1s in each group of bits. Let us assume our group of bits (which we will now refer to as a *binary number*) contains seven binary digits; for example:

$$1 \quad 0 \quad 0 \quad 1 \quad 0 \quad 1 \quad 1$$

If the system uses even parity then the parity bit needs to be **0** since there is already an even number of 1s.

However, if the system uses odd parity, then the parity bit needs to be **1** since we must have an odd number of 1s. Our *binary number* before transmission then becomes:

parity bit

either   **0 1 0 0 1 0 1 1**   for even parity

or   **1 1 0 0 1 0 1 1**   for odd parity

At the receiving end, the number of 1s is again totaled and if it is not even for an even parity system, then an error has occurred; if it isn't odd for an odd parity system, then again an error has occurred.

(i) What is the parity bit for the following binary number which uses even parity:

            ----- **1 1 1 0 1 1 0**

(ii) What is the parity bit for the following binary number which uses odd parity:

            ----- **0 0 1 0 1 1 0**

If two bits have been changed after transmission, it is possible for this parity check to fail to find the error. For example, using the above binary number again, **0 1 0 0 0 1 1 1** is clearly incorrect, but the parity still shows up as even and the parity check *wouldn't* detect an error in this case.

Very often *parity blocks* are used to help identify where an error has occurred. In this method, a block of data is sent and the number of 1s are added vertically and horizontally in an attempt to locate an error at the receiving end.

For example, suppose seven binary numbers have just been transmitted and an even parity check is being used by the system. A *parity byte* is also sent along with the seven binary numbers. This parity byte consists entirely of additional parity bits found from a vertical parity check on the seven binary numbers and is usually sent to indicate the end of the data block.

Now suppose the transmitted data has arrived as follows (each binary number sent is shown as row 1 to row 7 together with the parity byte).

	parity bit	column 2	column 3	column 4	column 5	column 6	column 7	column 8
row 1	1	0	1	1	0	1	1	1
row 2	1	1	0	0	1	1	0	0
row 3	0	1	1	0	0	0	1	1
row 4	0	1	0	0	0	0	0	1
row 5	1	0	0	0	1	1	1	1
row 6	1	1	1	1	0	0	0	0
row 7	0	0	0	1	0	0	0	1
parity byte:	0	0	1	0	0	1	1	1

It is clear from the above data that row 5 has an incorrect odd parity (five 1s) and column 4 also has an incorrect odd parity (three 1s). The intersection of row 5 and column 4 gives us the incorrect bit value (**0** in this case). It is therefore possible to change this bit value to **1** and produce the correct binary numbers. Alternatively, an error message is sent to the sending computer to request the data to be re-sent.

Automatic repeat request (ARQ)

Automatic repeat request (ARQ) is an error-control method used during data transmission. It makes use of **acknowledgements** (messages sent by a receiver indicating that data has been received correctly) and **timeouts** (the time period allowed to elapse before an acknowledgement is to be received).

If the sender does not receive an acknowledgement before the timeout, then the data is usually re-transmitted automatically.

Checksum

Checksums are also used to check if data has been corrupted during transmission. This can be determined in one of two ways. For consistency, we will assume here that the checksum of a block of data is 1 byte in length. This would give a maximum value of 255 since 00000000 can effectively be ignored. If the sum of the other bytes in the transmitted data block is 255 or less, then the checksum will contain the exact value.

However, if the sum of the other bytes in the block exceeds 255, then the checksum is found from the remainder of this total value after it has been divided by 256. For example:

- let us assume that the byte total is 1107
- 1107/256 gives the value 4.3242 (which is rounded to nearest whole number of 4)
- 4 x 256 equals 1024
- 1107 – 1024 gives 83 which is the checksum value.

Key Point	**Verification does not check if data makes any sense or is within acceptable boundaries; it only checks to see that data entered is identical to data on the original document.**

10.4   Binary Systems

The binary system is based on the number 2. This means that only the values 0 and 1 can be used to represent a digit in a binary number.

The binary headings will be powers of 2, i.e. 2^0 (1), 2^1 (2), 2^2 (4), 2^3 (8), 2^4 (16) and so on. A typical 8-digit binary number would be:

2^7	2^6	2^5	2^4	2^3	2^2	2^1	2^0
128	64	32	16	8	4	2	1
0	1	1	0	1	1	1	0

Conversion of binary to denary

The above binary number is equivalent to the denary (base 10) number 110. This was found by adding up each of the headings where a binary value of 1 appeared, i.e.

$$64 + 32 + 8 + 4 + 2 = 110$$

Conversion from denary to binary

To convert from denary into binary, it is a simple matter of placing 1s in the appropriate place until the denary number is reached. The unoccupied places are then filled with 0s.

For example, the denary value of 95 in binary is as follows:

128	64	32	16	8	4	2	1
0	1	0	1	1	1	1	1

Another method to find the binary number is to do successive division by 2. Using the same value of 95 we get the following:

2	95	
2	47	remainder 1
2	23	remainder 1
2	11	remainder 1
2	5	remainder 1
2	2	remainder 1
2	1	remainder 0
2	0	remainder 1
	0	remainder 0

> **Reading from the bottom to the top gives the binary number:**
>
> **0 1 0 1 1 1 1 1**
>
> **which is the same as in the first method shown above.**

The *memory size* of a computer is measured in terms of the number of *bytes*. A byte is usually referred to as 8 *binary digits (bits)*. Thus, a typical byte could be:

$$0\ 1\ 1\ 1\ 0\ 0\ 0\ 1$$

The memory size of a computer increases in multiples of 2. Thus,

1 kilobyte (kByte)	=	2^{10} bytes	=	1 024 bytes
1 megabyte (MByte)	=	2^{20} bytes	=	1 048 576 bytes
1 gigabyte (GByte)	=	2^{30} bytes	=	1 073 741 824 bytes
1 terabyte (TByte)	=	2^{40} bytes	=	1 099 511 627 776 bytes

and so on.

Some confusion exists around these terms since the IEC convention is now sometimes adopted. Manufacturers of computer storage devices tend to use denary values for memory; thus 1 kilobyte means 1 000 bytes, 1 megabyte means 1 000 000 bytes and so on. For this reason, the IEC convention uses the following new terms:

1 kibibyte (KiB)	=	1 024 bytes
1 mebibyte (MiB)	=	1 048 576 bytes
1 gibibyte (GiB)	=	1 073 741 824 bytes
1 tebibyte (TiB)	=	1 099 511 627 776 bytes

But these IEC terms are not universally used and would not be used in this textbook nor are you likely to see them in questions in the foreseeable future.

Within the processor unit there are areas known as ***registers*** which have a number of uses. A register is a group of bits in the computer memory, such as:

1	0	1	1	1	1	0	0

All data must be put into a register before it can be processed – refer to chapter 12 for more details on how this works.

The following example shows how registers can be used in a number of applications.

A car manufacturing company uses robots to spray their new cars with paint. A special edition model is being made which is only available in four colours and two paint finishes (metallic and non-metallic).

An 8-bit register is used to determine whether it is alright to paint the car and to choose the correct paint colour and finish.

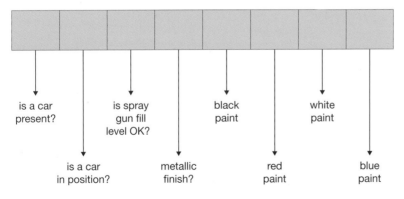

Note that all the above conditions give a 1 value; otherwise 0 value.

Computer Science Revision Guide
Cambridge IGCSE Computer Science Revision Guide

Thus, if an 8-bit register contains:

1	1	1	1	0	1	0	0

This means a car is present, car is in position, spray gun fill level is OK, and metallic red paint finish is chosen.

(i)   So what is represented by the following two 8-bit registers?

1	1	0	1	0	0	0	1
0	0	1	0	0	0	0	0

(ii)   What would be in the 8-bit register if the following conditions occurred?
Car is present but not in correct position, spray gun fill level is OK and non-metallic white paint has been chosen.

Answers

(i)   First register – car present, in position but a fault in spray gun fill level; metallic blue paint chosen.
Second register – no car present (and therefore not in position), and no paint colour or paint finish selected.

(ii)   Register contains: **1 0 1 0 0 0 1 0**

10.5   Hexadecimal systems

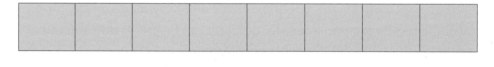

Hexadecimal (base 16) systems are allied very closely to the binary system. Since $16 = 2^4$ then one hexadecimal digit can be represented by four binary bits.

Hexadecimal system (hex system)

Hexadecimal (hex) is based on the number 16. Therefore 16 values need to be used to represent each digit in a hexadecimal number. The digits are represented by the numerical values 0 to 9 and the letters A to F (where A = 10, B = 11, C = 12, D = 13, E = 14 and F = 15).

The headings in a hexadecimal number will be powers of 16, i.e. 16^0 (1), 16^1 (16), 16^2 (256), 16^3 (4096) and so on. Therefore, a typical 5 digit hexadecimal number would be:

16^4	16^3	16^2	16^1	16^0
65536	4096	256	16	1
4	A	F	0	5

It was mentioned earlier on that each hexadecimal digit is equal to four binary digits. This fact is used extensively in the following examples.

Conversion of hexadecimal to binary

To convert hexadecimal to binary, it is necessary to first find the 4-bit binary equivalent to each hexadecimal digit.

So, the hexadecimal number   3   A   D   in binary becomes:

                    8 4 2 1   8 4 2 1   8 4 2 1
                    0 0 1 1   1 0 1 0   1 1 0 1

(NOTE: remember that A = 10 and D = 13)

Putting the digits together gives the binary number: 0 0 1 1 1 0 1 0 1 1 0 1

Conversion of hexadecimal to denary

To convert a hexadecimal number to denary, use the hexadecimal headings as follows:

          3   A   D

(3 x 256 = 768)   (10 x 16 = 160)   (13 x 1 = 13)

This gives the denary value of (768 + 160 + 13) 9 4 1

Conversion of binary to hexadecimal

To convert from binary to hexadecimal, divide up each binary number into groups of four digits starting from the RIGHT HAND side. If the final group has less than four digits then fill up with 0s. Then write down the hexadecimal value of each group of four digits.

Example 1

                1 1 1 0 0 0 0 1 1 1 1 0

            1 1 1 0   0 0 0 1   1 1 1 0

Hexadecimal digits: E   1   7

Example 2:

               1 1 1 1 0 0 1 1 1 1 0 0 1 0

          0 0 1 1   1 1 0 0   1 1 1 1   0 0 1 0

Hexadecimal digits: 3   C   F   2

Conversion of denary to hexadecimal

When converting from denary to hexadecimal, there are two common methods which involve either 'trial and error' or 'successive division by 16'.

Trial and error

With this method, you simply put hexadecimal digits in the appropriate column until the denary number is represented. For example: convert the number **2639** to hexadecimal:

256	16	1
A	**4**	**F**

(256 x 10) + (16 x 4) + (1 x 15)

Successive division by 16

16	2639	
16	164	remainder 15 (i.e. F)
16	10	remainder 4
	0	remainder 10 (i.e. A)

> **Reading from the bottom to the top gives the hexadecimal number:**
>
> **A 4 F**
>
> **which is the same as in the first method shown above.**

So why do we use hexadecimal (hex)?

Since 8 bits can be represented by only 2 hexadecimal digits or 16 bits by only 4 hexadecimal digits, it is easier for a human being to use the hexadecimal notation.

There are a number of areas where the hexadecimal notation is used. For example:

- memory dumps
- HTML
- MAC addresses
- assembly code/machine code

Memory dumps

If there is an error in a program or systems software, it is useful to carry out a *memory dump*. This is basically the contents of a section of computer memory. The contents of a number of memory locations are output in hexadecimal format. For example:

100FF110	6F 51 20 4E B1 38 2F 31 0C 0E 20 A1 2F 32 1F 23 20 15 3F 66
100FF117	20 36 41 51 EE E1 3F 4F 3E 20 A6 54 61 23 20 18 6D 68 65 64
100FF129	17 64 57 60 60 60 60 60 15 15 1F 20 20 20 20 20 20 20 20 20

The software engineer can now look at the memory dump and find out where the error lies. Using hexadecimal values makes this task much easier and quicker to carry out.

HTML (hypertext markup language)

Hypertext markup language (HTML) is used to write content on web pages; it is a markup language and not a programming language. HTML makes use of *<tags>*; there must be a beginning tag and an ending tag to make the code display correctly. For example,

<OL> starts an organised list

<(/OL)> ends an organised list

HTML code makes use of hexadecimal when representing colours on the screen. For example:

> # FF 00 00 represents the primary colour red
> # 00 FF 00 represents the primary colour green
> # 00 00 FF represents the primary colour blue.

Combinations of the above can be used to represent other colours, for example, # FF FF 00 represents yellow (red and green). It is possible to vary the hex values to create any colour the user wants. For example:

> # 41 69 E1 represents royal blue
> # 00 7F 00 represents lime green
> # CC CC CC represents light grey …. and so on.

MAC (media access control) addresses

A *media access control (MAC) address* is a unique number associated with network interface cards which identify a particular machine or device. This allows all devices to uniquely identify themselves on a computer network, for example, the Internet.

This address usually consists of 48 bits which are usually represented as 12 hexadecimal digits in the form:

MM – MM – MM – SS – SS – SS   or   MM:MM:MM:SS:SS:SS

where the first six hex digits represent the identification number of the manufacturer of the device and the second six hex digits represent the serial number of the device.

For example:

00 – A0 – C9 – 25 – F4 – 3D represents a device manufactured by Intel with a serial number of 25F43D.

Assembly language and machine code

Memory locations can be addressed directly using assembly language or machine code. This makes it much easier for programmers to write the code since using binary would be very cumbersome, very slow to write and would also increase the risk of errors. For example, it is much easier to write:

> ADD A7F4

than:

> ADD 1010 0111 1111 0100

10.6   End of chapter questions

10.6.1 Describe **four** methods used for automatic data capture. Give a different application for **each** of the methods chosen.

10.6.2 A record contains the following fields.

- Title (i.e. Mr, Mrs, Miss or Ms)

- Gender (i.e. M or F)

- Date of birth (for example, 15/10/1984)

- Pay number (i.e. must be nine digits long)

- Telephone number (for example, 0 131 216 5193)

- Pay per month (in $, highest pay is $20 000 per month)

When a new record is created, a user completes an on-screen form which contains all of the above fields (all of which are mandatory).

Describe a different validation check for **each** of the above 6 fields.

10.6.3 A system uses the ISBN-10 (modulus 11) method to generate check digits to validate barcode numbers on the back cover of books.

The check digit is calculated as follows:

- each digit in the barcode number is multiplied by its digit position

- the result of each multiplication is added to a total

- the final total is divided by 11

- the remainder after division, if any, is subtracted from 11 to give the check digit (if check digit = 10 this is shown as an 'X').

(a)   Which of the following barcode numbers have correct check digits? (please show all your working)

- 0 – 4 5 4 – 3 0 0 6 2 – X

- 0 – 2 1 2 – 9 1 1 3 4 – X

(b)   Calculate the check digits for the following barcode numbers (please show all your working).

- 0 – 5 5 5 – 2 1 5 3 3 – ?

- 0 – 1 2 1 – 9 0 0 2 1 – ?

(c)   Discuss the types of errors during data transmission which can be detected by using check digits.

10.6.4 (a)   Discuss **two** ways of carrying out verification checks.

(b)   How does verification differ from validation?

10.6.5 Hexadecimal (base 16) is a number system.

(a) Convert the following into binary.

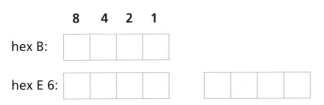

	8	4	2	1
hex B:				

| hex E 6: | | | | | | | | | |

(b) What hexadecimal numbers are represented by the following 12-bit register?

1	0	1	1	0	1	1	0	1	1	1	1

10.6.6 A burglar alarm system uses an 8-bit register. The first four bits indicate if a sensor has picked up an intruder (shown by a 1 value) and the second four bits indicate the zone where the sensor has picked up the intruder.

> **HINT:** split the register up into four 3-bit registers and then into three 4-bit registers before converting into hexadecimal.

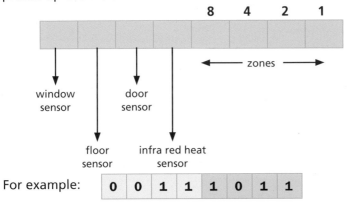

For example:

0	0	1	1	1	0	1	1

indicates the following: *door sensor and infra red heat sensors detected an intruder in zone 10 (8 + 2).*

(a) What is indicated by the following two registers?

0	1	0	1	0	1	1	1

1	0	0	0	1	1	0	0

(b) What would be the binary pattern for a window broken (picked up by window sensor) and infra red heat sensor detecting an intruder both in zone 15?

10.6.7 A car has a speedometer with a digital read out. Each digit can be represented by a 4-bit register.

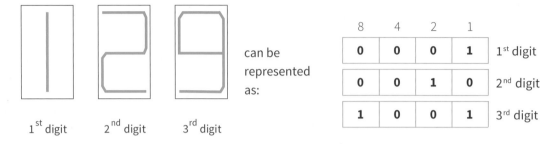

(a) What values must be in the 4-bit registers to represent the following speed shown on the speedometer?

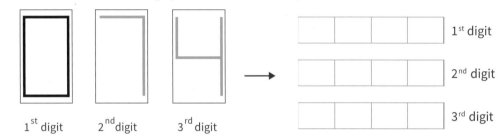

(b) What is shown on the digital speedometer if the 4-bit registers contain the following values:

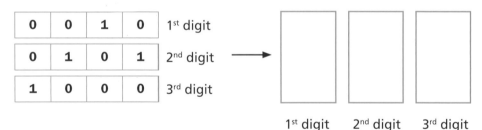

(c) If there was an error in the system, how could this be shown on the digital displays?

10.6.8 Eight chemical processes are being controlled by a computer. Each process also has eight inputs of chemicals.

One 4-bit register (A) is used to control the eight processes; a second 4-bit register (B) is used to control the addition of the chemicals. Thus:

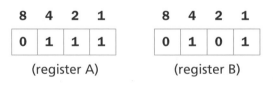

means *process 7 is under control (A) and chemical 5 is being added (B)*.

(a) What process control is being shown here:

8	4	2	1		8	4	2	1
0	1	1	1		0	1	0	1

     (register A)   (register B)

(b) What must be stored in the two registers (A and B) if process 3 is being controlled and chemical 6 is being added?

(c) 64 sensors were used to measure temperature of all the chemical inlets. The sensor number is represented in a 7-bit register.

An 8th bit is used to show if the sensor reading is acceptable (a 1 value means the temperature is acceptable; a 0 value means the temperature is not acceptable).

Thus, the following 8-bit register:

	64	32	16	8	4	2	1
1	0	1	1	0	1	1	1

means: *sensor 55 reading is acceptable.*

(i) What is the situation if the register is showing:

0	0	1	1	0	1	1	1

(ii) Show the binary values in the 8-bit register if thermometer 51 is showing a temperature which is not acceptable.

(iii) If the reading on the 8-bit register was:

1	0	1	1	0	0	1	0

What would be the equivalent hexadecimal numbers?

10.6.9 (a) Convert hexadecimal numbers B 0 F into denary.

    (b) Convert the denary number 3000 into *hex* notation.

    (c) Describe two reasons why hexadecimal numbers are used in computer systems.

10.6.10 (a) Explain what is meant by the term *even parity*.

    (b) Describe a situation where a parity check wouldn't identify an error in some data after it has been corrupted following transmission from one computer to another.

    (c) The following data block has been received by a computer.

      (even parity is used by the sending and receiving computer)

	Parity bit	col 2	col 3	col 4	col 5	col 6	col 7	col 8
row 1	1	0	0	1	1	1	0	0
row 2	0	0	0	0	1	1	0	0
row 3	0	1	1	1	1	0	1	1
row 4	1	0	0	0	0	0	0	1
row 5	1	1	1	0	1	1	0	1
row 6	1	1	1	1	0	0	0	0
row 7	1	1	1	0	1	0	0	1
parity byte	1	1	0	1	1	1	1	0

     (i)   Identify the bit which was corrupted after data transmission.

    (ii)   Give a reason for your choice.

(d)   Describe another method that could be used to detect corruption of data following transmission from one computer to another.

11 Hardware

Learning Summary

In this chapter you will learn about:
- *Features of laptop and desktop computers*
- *Household appliances*
- *Input and output devices*
- *Computer memories*

We have already considered software and a number of application areas. We will now consider the hardware itself which includes the computers, input/output devices and memories.

11.1 Features of laptop and desktop computers

Laptop/notebook computers have the obvious advantage over desktop computers (often referred to as PCs) in that they are extremely portable. This is because the screen, battery, keyboard and touchpad (equivalent to a mouse) are all integrated into one single package.

To be fully portable, these computers usually come with WiFi (wireless) technology which means that the user can take them anywhere and 'surf the net' or read/write emails provided there is a WiFi 'hot spot' nearby.

The usual considerations when buying laptop/notebook computers are the same as desktop computers, i.e. fast processors, size of RAM, number of USB ports, hard disk size and so on.

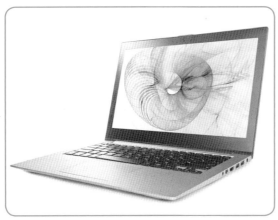

Laptop

But because the main advantage of laptop/notebook computers is their 'go anywhere' capability, there are certain additional features which are deemed to be very important:

– the processor should consume as little power as possible thereby prolonging internal battery life
– the processor should run as cool as possible minimising the problems associated with heat dissipation
– no fans needed to cool the processor thus reducing the load on the internal battery
– lightweight which makes the laptop/notebook completely portable.

With modern LCD screens and solid state memories, laptop/notebook computers are becoming thinner and much lighter in weight; they also consume less and less power reducing heat generation and further prolonging battery life. The advantage of laptop/notebook computers is clearly their portability making them almost indispensable to business users. However, compared to desktop computers, they do have some disadvantages.

Disadvantages

- They tend to be more expensive to purchase than desktop computers.
- Due to their portability, they are easier to steal.
- They tend to have a lower specification than the equivalent desktop computer (i.e. memory size and processor power).
- Greater security risks if sensitive data is stored on the hard drive.

A netbook has no CD/DVD writer, lower processor speed, etc.

A *netbook* is another type of portable computer. These are similar to laptop/notebook computers but are even smaller and lighter and have fewer features but are very useful for reading/sending emails, using the Internet, etc.

11.2 Household appliances

Many household devices make use of microprocessors to control their functions. A number of common devices are considered in this section, but this list is by no means exhaustive.

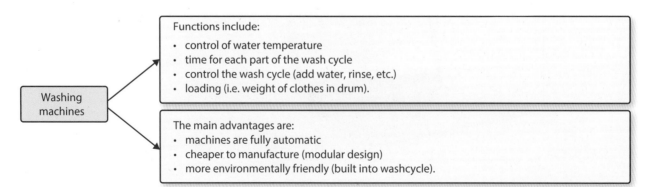

Washing machines

Functions include:
• control of water temperature
• time for each part of the wash cycle
• control the wash cycle (add water, rinse, etc.)
• loading (i.e. weight of clothes in drum).

The main advantages are:
• machines are fully automatic
• cheaper to manufacture (modular design)
• more environmentally friendly (built into washcycle).

Functions include:

- shutter speed
- lens focussing (sharpness of image)
- control of flash (automatically set off flask, etc.)
- aperture.

The main features include:

- the sensitivity of the camera depends on the number of pixels used to represent the photo taken (for example, 12 megapixel camera takes a sharper image than an 8 megapixel camera)
- the camera memory size also dictates how many photos can be taken (or it can allow more photos if the resolution is reduced, for example)
- sharpness of the image also depends very much on the camera lens quality.

Digital cameras

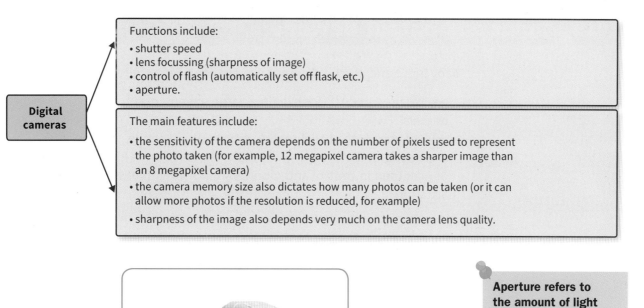

Digital camera

Aperture refers to the amount of light entering camera.

The advantages of digital cameras compared to traditional cameras include no processing costs as there is no film to develop and no photos to print out. It is easier to delete unwanted photos and to transfer them to an electronic form. It is much easier to modify the photos after they have been taken as considerable amount of software exists allowing the photographer to modify the photographs (colour, removal of unwanted parts of the image, etc.).

Functions include:

- automatic tuning into television stations
- allows digital signals to be decoded
- constantly monitor signals leading to better sound and picture quality
- allows interface with many devices (for example, games machines)
- built in diagnostics in case of malfunction
- modular design (easier maintenance)
- microprocessors allow stereo sound, 3D broadcast.

Television sets

The main features include:

- signals to televisions are now digital so it is essential to have microprocesors to interpret and decode these signals
- microprocessors are needed to control the complex functioning of plasma or LCD screens.

11.3 Input and output devices

Many input and output devices have already been covered in this book:

– devices used in CAD (for example, large screens, graph plotters, 3D ink jet printers)
– devices used with virtual reality systems (for example, data goggles, and data gloves)
– devices used in control and monitoring (for example, sensors, ADC/DAC, actuators).

This section will now cover some of the more common devices which are generally seen in the day to day operation of most computer systems.

Output devices

Printers

The most common type of printers are the dot matrix, inkjet and laser.

Dot matrix printer

These are old technology and are impact printers using an inked ribbon. They are still used in a number of areas because of their advantages and unique features. The following is a list of advantages and disadvantages of dot matrix printers.

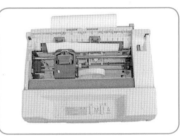

Dot matrix printer

Advantages

- They work with continuous (fan folded) stationery which means they can do very large print jobs without any human interaction.
- They work with multi-part stationery which means 'carbon copies' can be made immediately.
- Relatively inexpensive to run and maintain.
- Can work in damp and dirty atmospheres – an environment which would cause problems for the other two printers.
- Able to print raised characters, i.e. braille to allow blind or partially-sighted people to read the outputs.

Disadvantages

- They are relatively expensive to purchase in the first place.
- They tend to be very noisy in operation.
- Printing is slow and usually of a very poor quality compared to laser and inkjet.
- Although they do work in colour (usually a 4-colour ribbon), the results are very limited.

Inkjet printer

Inkjet printers are made up of:

- a *print head* which consists of nozzles used to spray droplets of ink
- an *ink cartridge* which contains special ink; this can be either one cartridge containing all the ink colours including black or a number of separate cartridges for each ink colour and black
- a *stepper motor* and *belt* which moves the print head assembly back and forth across the page
- *paper feed* which feeds single sheets of paper automatically into the printer body.

So what happens when the user selects OK to print? The following flow diagram shows the stages in the printing process.

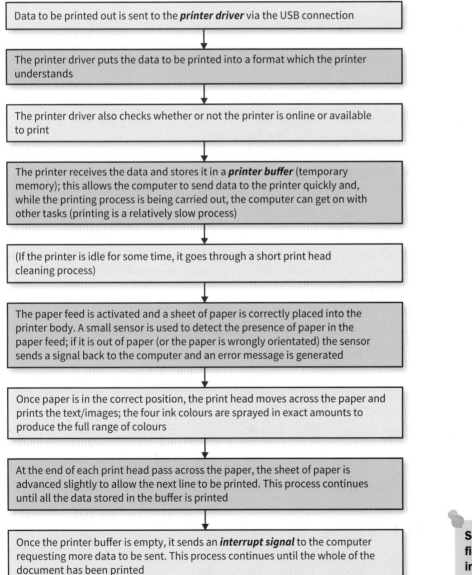

Data to be printed out is sent to the ***printer driver*** via the USB connection
The printer driver puts the data to be printed into a format which the printer understands
The printer driver also checks whether or not the printer is online or available to print
The printer receives the data and stores it in a ***printer buffer*** (temporary memory); this allows the computer to send data to the printer quickly and, while the printing process is being carried out, the computer can get on with other tasks (printing is a relatively slow process)
(If the printer is idle for some time, it goes through a short print head cleaning process)
The paper feed is activated and a sheet of paper is correctly placed into the printer body. A small sensor is used to detect the presence of paper in the paper feed; if it is out of paper (or the paper is wrongly orientated) the sensor sends a signal back to the computer and an error message is generated
Once paper is in the correct position, the print head moves across the paper and prints the text/images; the four ink colours are sprayed in exact amounts to produce the full range of colours
At the end of each print head pass across the paper, the sheet of paper is advanced slightly to allow the next line to be printed. This process continues until all the data stored in the buffer is printed
Once the printer buffer is empty, it sends an ***interrupt signal*** to the computer requesting more data to be sent. This process continues until the whole of the document has been printed

See chapter 12 to find out how these interrupts work.

The ink droplets are currently produced by two different types of technology:

Thermal bubble   – with this technology, tiny resistors create localised heat which vaporises the ink creating a bubble. As the bubble expands, some ink is ejected from the print head onto the paper. When the bubble collapses, a vacuum is formed and fresh ink is pulled into the print head ready for more printing.

Piezoelectric   – with this technology, a crystal is located at the rear of the ink reservoir for each nozzle. The crystal receives a small electric charge which makes it vibrate. The vibration causes ink to be ejected onto the paper and also draws in more ink for further printing.

Advantages

- Inkjet printers are very cheap to purchase in the first place.
- They produce high quality output; used to produce photographs.
- Relatively quiet in operation.

Disadvantages

- Ink cartridges do not last very long – which makes the printer unsuitable for any long print runs.
- Printing can 'smudge' if touched too early or the wrong paper type is used.
- Relatively expensive to run.

> **The increased cost is mainly due to ink cartridges.**

Laser printers

Laser(jet) printers make use of the properties of static electricity to enable printing on paper to take place. A **printing drum** is given a **positive charge** and, as the drum rotates, the printer scans a laser beam across the surface of the drum removing the positive charge in certain places. This process allows the laser to recognise letters or images to be printed as **electrostatic images.**

The printer then coats the drum with positively charged toner (powdered ink). Since this toner is positive, it only sticks to the **negatively charged** areas on the drum (i.e. those areas where the positive charge has been discharged). The drum then rolls over a sheet of paper which has been given a negative charge. This negative charge is bigger than the negative charge on the electrostatic image; consequently, toner powder leaves the drum and sticks to the paper instead. To prevent the paper sticking to the drum it has its charge removed immediately after the printing process.

Finally, the paper goes through a **fuser** which is basically a set of heated rollers. The heated rollers melt the ink which fixes it permanently to the paper. A discharge lamp then removes all the charge from the drum making it ready for the next page to be printed.

Laser printers have a number of advantages and disadvantages.

Advantages

- They have very low noise levels.
- Fast output and well suited to high volume printing.
- Toner cartridges last a long time.
- Print quality is extremely good.

Disadvantages

- Maintenance and running costs can be expensive (for example, colour toner cartridges and replacement of diffuser packs are expensive). Printing can 'smudge' if touched too early or the wrong paper type is used.
- They produce ozone and volatile organic matter which can be harmful to some people when the printer is used in an office environment.

> **Laser printers are more cost effective when compared to inkjet printers.**

3D inkjet printers (stereolithography printers)

These printers are primarily used in CAD applications and actually produce 3D solid objects. The technology uses a modified inkjet printer and the object is built up layer by layer until the solid object is produced. The material used in the printer to make the thin layers can be plaster, resin, concrete, plastics, metal, etc. Some new developments are using laser printers rather than inkjet printers; but the principle behind the technology is the same in both cases.

> **It is based on the *tomography* principle which involves breaking down any object into a series of thin layers.**

Researchers are using 3D printers to produce artificial bones for use in facial reconstruction surgery.

Solid bone structure produced on a 3D printer as part of medical research

A 3D computer model of the bone is created based on patients' X-ray and CT scan. The computer model is then sliced up (tomography) into a number of thin slices; this data is sent to a 3D inkjet printer which uses powdered α – tricalcium phosphate instead of paper and the 'ink' is a polymer which hardens on contact. The printer builds up the bone structure by printing successive layers on top of each other. There is still much research to be done here and in other medical applications (making artificial teeth, arteries, etc.), but this is a very interesting field which could produce dramatic results in the next decade or so.

As the cost of 3D (stereolithography) printers continues to fall, continued research will eventually allow owners to 'print out' metal parts for cars or even printed circuit boards for computers.

Printer applications

The choice of which printer to use is very important in any application.

3D printers

3D printers are used in any application where a working prototype/model needs to be made. They are being used increasingly in a number of applications where other methods are very expensive or even impossible.

Examples include:

- creation of museum artefacts (i.e. copies of ancient statues, pottery, jewellery and so on which would be difficult to do by any other method); the artefact is scanned using a 3D scanner which produces a tomographic image (i.e. made up of several thousand slices – see later); the images are processed by 3D software and then sent to a 3D printer where an accurate replica in resin, powdered stone, powdered metal or plastic is produced
- production of parts for a vintage car; since these parts are no longer available, this is often the only way to obtain parts for a reasonable price; either the original part is scanned as above or a blueprint is produced using CAD software; an actual working part in metal is then produced; in many cases, the customer simply sends the file to a company who operate industrial 3D printers and the design is 'printed out' for them.

Dot matrix printers

Dot matrix printers are old technology but still have a use in the 21st century. They can operate in atmospheres which are hostile to inkjet or laser printers, for example, damp or dusty/dirty atmospheres in factories. The use of multi-part, continuous stationery is also a very useful feature for certain applications. For example:

- when producing wage/salary slips, dot matrix printers are still regarded as very useful; they can print through paper which is; 'carbonised' so that the printing is on the inside of the document and can't be read from the outside. This works because the printer is an impact printer and doesn't need to be in actual contact with the paper to do the printing (unlike laser and inkjet).

 The first layer is security paper (can't be seen through)
The second layer is carbon (to produce the printing when it receives an impact)
The third layer is the blank paper which is printed on during the process
The fourth layer is again security paper.

The printer impacts on one of the security layers to produce the printing

The paper is on a continuous so that the wage/salary slips are produced hundreds at a time and then each one is torn off at the perforations to produce a secure wage/salary slip.

The image on the right shows a typical security layer on a wage/salary slip; the dot matrix printer prints through this onto a sheet of paper inside; because of the pattern on the security sheet, it is impossible to read what is printed inside.

Inkjet printers

Inkjet printers are generally used where one-off high quality printing needs to be done – for example, production of a document with colour images and text.

They are also excellent at producing photographs because of the nature of the printing used and can therefore be used on glossy paper.

Laser printers

Laser printers are used where high speed printing or large volume printing is required. Because laser printers have large paper trays (often holding more than 1000 sheets) and large toner cartridges, they are better suited to big print runs (inkjet printers usually have a small paper tray and use very small ink cartridges). An inkjet printer would quickly run out of paper and would need frequent changing of ink cartridges on a run involving several hundred sheets of paper. Because of the way they operate, they are much faster at producing duplicate copies of a particular page (or pages).

Monitors
Cathode ray tube (CRT) monitors

These types of monitors are being phased out, not only due to their bulk and weight, but also because their power consumption is very high. They also 'flicker' as they get older giving rise to headaches if used for any length of time. In spite of all this, they do have two main advantages:

– image quality is probably still better than the equivalent TFT monitor
– at the moment, only CRTs can be used with light pens (due to the high speed electron beam and screen refresh every 85 times a second, so many design offices still use CRT monitors for this reason.

This difference is diminishing as the TFT technology improves.

Thin-film transistor (TFT) monitors

TFT monitor

These monitors use thin-film transistor technology. The screen is made up of thousands of tiny pixels; each pixel has three transistors coloured red, green and blue and the intensity of each determines the colour seen by the human eye. TFT monitors have a number of advantages when compared to CRT monitors.

> Some newer versions now use 4-colour transistors with a yellow one added to further improve the colour definition.

> TFT screen can now be fitted into a desktop and used in the same way you would read a book or document.

Advantages

- They are very light weight.
- They consume very little power and also have less screen glare.
- They increase the flexibility of the computer system.
- The only problem is the viewing angle which needs to be considered when using a TFT screen to display some information; a CRT screen may be the best option in certain applications.

Many *liquid crystal display (LCD)* monitors now also incorporate *light emitting diode (LED)* technology. Such monitors consist of a front layer of LCD (liquid crystal diode/display) that makes up the image from a number of pixels. This LCD layer is then back-lit using LEDs which give it better brightness and contrast. LEDs have several advantages over the older CCFC (cold cathode fluorescent lamp) technology used to back-lit LCD monitors in the past:

- they reach their maximum brightness almost immediately (no need to 'warm up')
- they give a 'whiter' tint sharpening the image and making it look more 'vivid'; CCFCs gave a yellowish tint
- they produce a brighter light than CCFCs allowing the picture to be much brighter in appearance
- the monitors are now much thinner due to the use of LEDs
- since LEDs last almost indefinitely, this technology is much more reliable and consistent
- since LEDs consume very little power, LCDs back-lit with this technology are very energy efficient.

Future LED development is considering *organic light emitting diodes (OLEDs).* The organic materials used to create the semiconductors are very flexible allowing displays which can be bent into any desired shape! Because of this aspect, OLEDs are expected to feature in future monitor, television and mobile phone screen advancements. This could, for example, allow somebody to fold up their full-sized computer monitor and carry it anywhere they want in their pocket! Clearly the possible applications of such technology are almost as limitless as the imagination.

2D and 3D cutters

A three-dimensional (3D) laser cut is similar to a two-dimensional (2D) cut except it is able to recognise the object in an x–y–z direction rather than in just an x–y direction. The materials which can be cut using 3D laser cutters include glass, crystal, metals, polymers and wood. This enables much more complex shapes to be cut.

3D cutters can go beyond the surface of the material being shaped and actually cut at the centre of the material.

Loud speakers

Essentially how sound is produced from a computer can be represented by a fairly simple diagrammatic representation.

The computer will send out a digital signal which is converted to an analogue voltage using a digital to analogue converter (DAC). This voltage is then amplified and then fed to a loud speaker. The voltage changes make a cone inside the loud speaker vibrate producing sounds.

This includes output devices such as loud speakers or head phones.

Light projectors

There are two common types of light projectors used to project multimedia onto a large screen or whiteboard. The common types are:

- Digital light projectors (DLPs), and
- Liquid crystal display (LCD) projectors.

Digital light projectors (DLPs)

Millions of tiny micro mirrors on a small *Digital light projector (DLP)* chip are key to the functioning of DLP technology.

The number and arrangement of micro mirrors in the DLP chip determines the resolution of the digital image. These micro mirrors can either tilt towards the light source (i.e. ON) or away from the light source (i.e. OFF) creating a light or dark pixel on the projection surface. Each of the micro mirrors can switch on or off several thousand times a second; for example, if the micro mirror switches ON more frequently than OFF, it produces a light grey pixel. Typically the micro mirrors can produce pixels in 1024 grey shades giving the video signal entering the DLP chip a *grey scale image.*

A white light source in the projector passes through a colour filter on its path to the DLP chip. This white light is split into the three primary colours: red, green and blue, from which a DLP projector can create well over 16 million different colours. The ON and OFF states of each of the DLP micro mirrors are then linked with the colours of the colour filter producing the coloured image. This concept is similar to black and white photography where grey scales on the photograph represent real life colours.

DLP technology is effectively reversing this concept and interpreting the generated shades of grey as actual colours.

It is suggested that the reader finds about the older LCD projectors and compares their performance to these DLP projectors.

LCD projectors

These are an older type of projector than the DLP variety. They are based on a high intensity beam of white light passing through an LCD display.

The light beam is sent to mirrors coated in a light sensitive material; when light is reflected back from the mirrors, its wavelength is changed (corresponding to red, green and blue light). The reflected light passes through three LCD screens (the image on the LCD screens is in the form of millions of pixels representing the image as a grey scale). When each of the three coloured beams of light pass through the LCD screens, they produce the grey scale image in red, green and blue format. Combining these coloured images produces the full colour image which is then projected onto the large screen or whiteboard.

Input devices

The most common examples of input devices include:

- keyboards/keypads
- pointing devices (for example, mouse, touchpad, trackerball, joystick)
- touch screens.

There are more specialist devices covered elsewhere in this book. For example:

→ Barcode readers used in supermarkets to read information about products (printed on barcodes) and for automatic stock control.
→ Scanners/OCR used to convert hard copy documents into an electronic form; OCR software allows the scanned text to be manipulated.

→ OMR can read pencil/pen marks in a pre-determined position on a script; used in questionnaires, multiple choice exam papers and so on.

→ MICR (Magnetic Ink Character Recognition) is used to read text printed in magnetic ink.

→ Digital cameras/webcams are used to capture images and download them directly to the computer; digital cameras have internal memories and can also save the images. However, webcams do not save the images and they are transmitted directly to the computer and tend to be used in online chatting or in video conferencing.

→ Microphones are used to capture sound/voices for use in voice overs in presentations, online chatting, allowing disabled users to input data into a computer.

Touch screens

Touch screens are similar to normal monitors but in this case allow selections (and other features) to be made by touching the screen rather than using a pointing device, such as a mouse.

When the screen is touched, sensitive layers on the screen convert the 'touch' into an electrical signal. Sensors can identify a touch has been made and a microprocessor is used to determine the position on the screen where the touch was made. They are commonly used in Information Centres.

> **Also see notes in chapter 2 regarding mobile phone touch screens.**

Information centres

Airports, bus stations, railway stations, supermarkets and any application where information needs to be relayed to customers on a regular basis, all gain benefit from having automatic (unmanned) information kiosks/desks. These allow customers to automatically obtain information as and when they require it without having to interface with human operators.

Output is normally on a large screen, but although the methods of input can vary, they are usually at least one of the following:

- touch screens with menu options
- mouse/trackerball to select options from a screen
- limited options keyboard/concept keyboard
- light pens when CRT screens are used.

Key Point	**Normal keyboards are not offered since the number of options is limited and the organisation does not want customers keying in other information or attempting to 'hack' into the system.**

Using these automatic information kiosks/desks located around an airport, bus, train station or supermarket would have the following advantages to the customers and the company.

Advantages

- The system can be linked into websites.
- The information is usually more up to date and accurate.
- There are no language problems as language options can be given on screen and the customer selects the most appropriate one; man-operated desks would have limited language capability.
- Customers do not have to wait in queues.
- Companies can advertise special offers, special services, immediate problems and so on.
- Lower overall costs to companies as fewer staff needed.
- The kiosks/desks are open 24/7 since they are unmanned.

These are a very useful option at airports, bus or railway stations where it is possible to have 'live' arrivals and departures boards.

Scanners

Scanners are used to input hard copy information into an electronic format which can be understood by a computer. When the document is placed on the glass plate in the scanner, a light is used to illuminate the document. A scan head then moves across the document and 'reads' the information converting it into a form understood by the computer. If the computer is equipped with *optical character recognition (OCR)* software, then text on the paper can be converted into a text file format. This can then be edited by importing the text file into software such as a word processor. Photographs and other images are often converted into a file format such as jpeg (see later).

3D scanners can convert physical objects into digital 3D data. These scanners capture the x-y-z coordinates at several points over the object being scanned to create a digital image. The scanned data can be converted into CAD software and then ultimately used in a CAD/CAM manufacturing process.

There are presently three common laser scanning techniques used in 3D scanners as shown here.

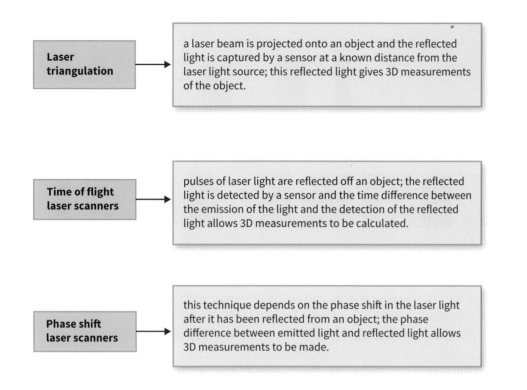

Sometimes white light scanning is used instead of laser lights. In this case, a known pattern of white light is projected onto an object and sensors detect the reflected light allowing an image to be built up. Examples of this include: *photogrammetry* (used to digitize large objects such as buildings) and *CT (computed tomography)/MRI (magnetic resonance imaging)* which break down an object into 'slices' (used in hospitals to scan human brains and whole body scans) so each slice can be analysed if required.

Use of scanners at airports

Passport scanners are now used at airports to scan data from passports. It uses OCR technology to provide high quality digital images of the scanned document in a format that can be understood by a computer. The data is usually stored in a database which allows easy searching and manipulation of the data. The system will automatically:

- identify a scanned document
- locate the required text and images
- carry out any required error detection
- store the text in an *ASCII file format* (common standard for storage of characters found on any computer keyboard; each character has unique binary pattern, for example, letter 'F' is represented as: 0100 0110 (46 hex)).

Barcode readers

Barcodes are made up of a series of black and white parallel lines of varying thickness. Each series of lines represents the code for the numbers

0 to 9. A number of different methods for representing these codes are used. The following shows one of these methods.

number: 2   number: 5

A barcode is made up of several of these codes.

numbers: 5   7   0   3

The following sequence shows how a typical barcode is read:

– a barcode reader shines an LED or red laser light onto the barcode to be scanned
– the light is reflected back off the barcode; the white lines reflecting more light
– the reflected light is detected by photoelectric cells (sensors)
– as the light is scanned over the barcode, it generates a pattern which can be interpreted by the computer:

for example, number 5 gives us: | W B B W WW B | (W = white, B = black)

or: | 0 1 1 0 0 0 1 | (binary equivalent)

– these binary codes can then be used by the computer for stock control, searching for items in stock, locating prices of items, identification of an item and so on.

Barcode technology is used in most supermarkets around the world at the checkouts where each barcode is scanned by a *barcode reader/scanner*. The barcode is looked up in a database (the barcode number is usually the key field for searching purposes) and once the required item is found, details such as price and description are sent back to the checkout (or *point of sale (POS) terminal*). The item is also 'flagged' as being sold and the new quantity in stock written back to the appropriate record in the database.

3D barcodes/QR codes

Another type of barcode is known as the **QR (Quick Response)** code. This is made up of a matrix of black squares on a white background.

The standard barcodes described above can hold up to 30 numbers; however, a QR barcode can hold over 7000 numbers which allows them to store massive amounts of data.

With the increase in Internet-enabled mobile phones, these QR codes can be easily scanned using an *application* previously downloaded to the

This quantity of stock is compared to the minimum order/stock level and if it is equal to this value, or less, then an automatic re-order for new stock is generated by the computer.

phone; this takes the user to a website or simply displays text or contact information on the phone. For example, QR code given here represents a 16-digit code (0194 3256 7111 2388), which could be the code for a holiday offer, and once scanned, the user will be sent to the holiday website or contact details/brief description of the holiday will appear on the screen.

Advantages

- There is no need to physically write down details. By simply scanning the QR code, the desired information is captured automatically by the mobile phone or other device.
- QR codes can be used to store addresses and URLs that can appear in magazines, on signs, buses, business cards or just about any product that users might need information about.

Disadvantages

- Users must be equipped with a camera phone and the correct reader application that can scan the image of the QR code. Currently only *smartphones* are technically capable of doing this.

Microphones

Microphones are used to pick up sound directly and input this data into a computer. Inside the microphone, a diaphragm vibrates according to the nature of the sound detected (volume, pitch, frequency and so on) and produces an electric signal. This signal goes to a *sound card* which converts the signal to a digital form (using a digital to analogue converter (DAC)) so that the computer can understand the data. The digital signals are recorded and now represent the sound originally detected by the microphone.

Microphones can be used to help people communicate with computer if they cannot operate devices such as keyboards or mouse. *Voice recognition software* is used to understand human spoken words and shows these words on a screen in much the same way as when a user types words on a keyboard. Voice recognition software compares the wave pattern of the spoken words and matches them to wave patterns stored in memory thus producing the text shown on the screen. This software is becoming increasingly sophisticated and produces far fewer errors, such as those caused by strong accents or dialects which 'confuse' the software by producing 'unusual' wave patterns.

> Microphones are usually either built-in or connected externally via a USB port.

Keyboard

Keyboards are probably the most common input device used on computers and other equipment such as mobile phones. The keyboard can be either a physical device connected via a USB port or by wireless (WiFi) or it can be a *virtual* device such as those used on many mobile phones. In the latter case, a keyboard appears on a touch screen and the user 'types' by gently touching the letter on the screen.

See earlier section on inkjet printers and also chapter 1.

Each character typed on the keyboard is converted into an electric signal which the computer interprets and stores in memory. Keyboard buffers are used since keyboard entry is very slow compared to the speed at which the processor works.

Mouse

The *mouse* is an example of a *pointing device* and is usually used with a GUI (graphical user interface) where items are selected and one of the mouse buttons 'clicked' to indicate what action the computer needs to take next. Applications of the mouse are mentioned throughout this textbook and are similar to touch screens in the way that information is conveyed to a computer.

As with keyboards, the mouse can either be connected directly via the USB port or wirelessly (WiFi).

The following section considers specialist input/output devices.

Interactive whiteboards

Interactive whiteboards are devices where users can actually write on the board and their text or drawings are automatically saved in an electronic form for later use. This is very useful at a meeting, for example, where a number of people may be involved in a discussion on some new product, for example.

It can be used in conjunction with computer output using software such as a spreadsheet, database, CAD, computer game and so on. Imagine a graph showing company profits over a 12-month period. The graph is projected on the whiteboard and the people at the meeting can annotate the graph and their comments can then be incorporated into a final report. Or the comments can simply be loaded a few days later from the device used to save the annotations electronically.

The following graph showing performance of a restaurant indicates a typical use of interactive whiteboards:

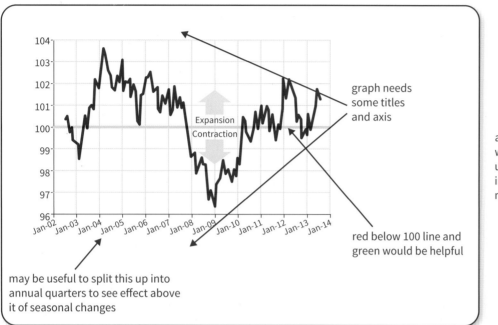

11.4   Memory, storage devices and media

Memory and *storage devices* can basically be split up into three categories.

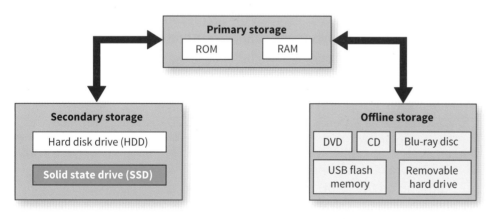

Primary storage

Random access memory (RAM)

Random access memory (RAM) has the following characteristics:

- they are *volatile* memories (i.e. the contents of the memory are lost on turning off the power to the computer)
- they store data, files, device drives and operating system *currently being used;* this is a temporary function
- these memories can be written to and read from; the contents can be changed by the user.

When the RAM fills up, the processor needs to continually access the hard disk to overlay old data in RAM with the new data; this inevitably slows down the operation of the computer. However, RAM *never* actually runs out of memory; it just keeps operating but read/write operations become slower and slower. Increasing the size of the RAM reduces the number of times the processor has to read data from the hard disk – an operation that takes much longer than reading data from RAM.

Buffers are usually composed of RAM chips. Printer buffers, CD/DVD read/write buffers and keyboard buffers all store data temporarily until the device is able to process the data (also refer to section 11.3). These buffers stop slower peripheral devices holding up computer operations (they compensate for the different operational speeds between the processor and devices such as a printer). This allows the processor to perform other tasks whilst, for example, printing out a document. Obviously, the larger the buffer, the less often it has to be serviced by the processor speeding up operations even further.

> **Task: find out how *double buffering* works and what are its advantages.**

Read only memory (ROM)

Read only memory (ROM) has the following characteristics:

– they are *non-volatile* memories (i.e. permanent since the contents are not lost when the power is turned off to the computer)
– the contents can be read only; it cannot be modified
– the ROM often holds the instructions for starting up the computer (for example, the *BIOS – basic input/output system*).

The access rate for ROM is less than the access rate for RAM; but RAM size is usually larger in the majority of computers. Another type of memory often described as primary memory is DVD-RAM.

DVD-RAM

DVD-RAM uses a different format to CD and DVD systems. They have the following features:

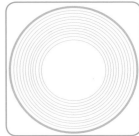

– they store data in concentric tracks (see drawing on the right) unlike CDs/DVDs which have *one* single spiral track
– the concentric track format enables data on the DVD-RAM to be written to and read from the disk at the same time
– the above features make DVD-RAM ideal for DVD recorders; early MP3 players often used mini DVD-RAMs to allow read/write operations to be done many times. A user could watch a television programme saved on the DVD-RAM at the same time as he recorded another programme; they also allow what is known as 'live pause' which allows a user to pause a tv programme being transmitted and then catch up later without missing any of the tv programme.

Secondary storage

(Fixed) Hard disk drive

Hard disk drive (HDD) is the main method used to store data in a computer; although this is rapidly being replaced by solid state systems.

They contain hard disks coated in a magnetic layer. Read/write heads close to the surface allow data to be written to and read from the disk surface. HDD systems are commonly used to store operating systems and applications software.

Solid state drives (SSDs)

Solid state technology is now used in many computers. *Solid state drive (SSD)* units are replacing fixed hard disk drives which are one of the main reasons why laptop computers are becoming thinner and lighter.

Instead of changing the magnetic properties on a magnetic surface layer, as is done on hard disk drives, solid state systems control the movement of electrons within a chip. The data is represented as 1s and 0s stored in millions of transistors within a chip. There are no moving parts and consequently SSDs are more robust and also consume much less power (which also means they run much cooler – a key feature in laptop design).

SSDs make use of NAND flash memories – these involve millions of transistors wired in series on a single circuit board and produce non-volatile, rewritable memories which are very light weight.

> **The reader is invited to find out how NAND flash memories tie up with NAND gates discussed in chapter 8.**

Offline storage

CD and DVD disks

These storage media are essentially different to hard disks and floppy disks in that they use the properties of light to read from/write data on a disk surface (known as *optical media*). A thin layer of metal alloy or organic dye is used as the *recording media*. CDs and DVDs have only *one spiral track* (see drawing on

the right). The data is stored in *pits* (spiral grooves that run from the centre of the disk to the edge. A red laser reads the other side of the pits, known as the *bumps*, to allow the data to be read. The letter 'R' after the CD or DVD (i.e. CD-R and DVD-R) means data can be read only once the disk has been *finalised*. The letters 'RW' (i.e. CD-RW and DVD-RW) mean data can be written to and read from the disk.

> **Due to *dual-layering* technology, the data capacity of a DVD is much greater than a CD.**

Blu-ray discs

Unlike normal DVDs, which use a **red laser** light to read/write data, *Blu-ray discs* use a **blue laser**. This has a much shorter wavelength (405 nanometres) than a red laser (650 nanometres). The smaller light beam can therefore focus more precisely enabling it to read data recorded in *pits* only 0.15 microns long, which is much smaller than the pits on normal DVDs. This technology allows Blu-ray discs to store up to five times more data than a DVD disk.

A Blu-ray disc is about the same thickness (1.2 mm) as a DVD, but the storage of data is very different:

- in a DVD, data is sandwiched between two 0.6 mm polycarbonate layers; this can lead to *birefringence* (where light is refracted into two separate beams thus preventing the DVD from being read)
- Blu-ray discs, however, store data on the top of a single 1.1 mm polycarbonate disk; this prevents *birefringence*
- Blu-ray discs also come equipped with a *secure encryption system* – a unique identification that prevents video piracy and copyright infringement.

It is worth comparing the specifications of the three most common optical media formats.

Optical media	Laser type	Construction	Track pitch (distance between each track)
CD	780 nm red laser	one 1.2 mm polycarbonate layer	1.60 μm
DVD	650 nm red laser	two 0.6 mm polycarbonate layers	0.74 μm
Blu-ray	405 nm blue laser	one 1.1 mm polycarbonate layer	0.30 μm

Memory sticks/pen drives/USB flash drives

Pen drive

Memory sticks (also known as pen drives and USB flash drives) are solid state technology (see earlier). They usually connect through the USB port from where they also obtain their power. Memory sticks are usually small, portable devices which do not require any additional software to run since most operating systems usually automatically recognise them as the E-drive,

F-drive and so on. They are often used by users as a form of back up for important files in case of any problems with the fixed hard drive system.

Many expensive software packages store security files on memory sticks which they supply with the software. These are known as *dongles* and must be present when the software is run. This prevents companies and individuals from using the software for unauthorised use.

Removable hard disk drives

Removable hard disk drives work in a similar way to fixed hard disk drives, but the main difference is that they are portable and usually connect to the computer through the USB port. The memory capacity of these devices seems to increase every year where 3 or 4 Tbytes is now a common size.

Data storage

Here we will consider MIDI (Musical Instrument Digital Interface) files, jpeg files, MP3 and MP4 files.

Musical instrument digital interface (MIDI)

The concept of *MIDI* is often confused. A MIDI file is NOT music and does not contain any sounds nor is it a music file like MP3. MIDI is actually nothing more than data that contains a list of messages that tell a device (such as a musical instrument, computer sound card or a mobile phone) *how* to generate a sound or music. Some examples of these messages are:

– 'note on' signals that a key has been pressed or a note from an instrument (such as a guitar) has been played
– 'note off' signals that a key has been released
– 'key pressure' signals how hard a key has been pressed.

> There are clearly many more messages and these just give a sample of those used.

When music is recorded on a computer using MIDI, the software saves the messages as a *.mid file*. When the file is played back on, for example, an electronic keyboard instrument, the keyboard's software follows the *.mid file* instruction to faithfully play back the musical notes. Any electronic instrument can be hooked up to the computer to play back the *.mid file*.

One advantage of using *.mid files* is that they do not contain actual music notes or sounds, so their file size is much smaller than MP3 or MP4 files. As an example, using MP3 format to store one minute of audio requires ~1 Mbyte file size; the same one minute of audio using MIDI format only requires ~10 Kbyte file size. This makes MIDI ideal for mobile ring tones, for example.

MP3 (MPEG-3) files/MP3 players

MPEG-3 (MP3) uses *audio compression* technology to convert audio to an MP3 format; normal music files on a CD are compressed by a factor of about 10 whilst retaining most of the music quality. For example, a 64 Mbyte music file is compressed to a 6.4 Mbyte MP3 file.

Music files in MP3 format are usually downloaded from a computer via USB port to an MP3 player. The MP3 player has its own battery which allows a user to listen to the music files through personal headphones or connected to an external sound amplification system.

The MP3 format makes use of **perceptual music shaping**, which removes sounds the human ear cannot hear properly. For example, if two sounds are being played, the MP3 format also only keeps the sound which is louder – the softer sound is discarded.

MP4 (MPEG-4) files/MP4 players

MPEG-4 (MP4) files are a format which allows multimedia rather than just audio files (as in MP3).

They work in a similar way to MP3, but they store audio, video, photo and animation files. They also allow streaming of multimedia files over the Internet. They work by compressing files without affecting the quality of, for example, the video by making certain aspects of the original file redundant.

JPEG (joint photographic experts group) files

Jpeg is an image encoding system that compresses photographs and other images. It is a *lossy* format and makes use of certain properties of human vision to eliminate certain unnecessary information.

It is a very complex process which goes way beyond the scope of this book. Putting it in simple terms, it relies on the human eye being unable to distinguish colours of similar brightness or similar hues. A typical RGB (red, green, blue) bit map image is converted to a YCbCr image (where Y = brightness of the pixel, Cb/Cr = chroma, which are the blue and red differences, respectively); these images are considerably smaller in size than the original.

Lossless and lossy compression

File compression can be termed either **lossless** or **lossy** in nature.

Lossless

Lossless file compression is based on the idea that files can be broken down into files of 'similar size' for transmission or storage, and then put back together again at the receiving end so it can be used again.

Lossy

Lossy file compression works differently to lossless file compression. Lossy compression algorithms eliminate unnecessary bits of information. It becomes impossible to get back to the original file once this lossy compression algorithm has been applied and the new file stored.

Refer to jpeg system described earlier, for example.

File compression software looks for redundancies in a file and eliminates these redundancies to reduce the file size. Some of the file compression formats have been covered earlier in this section.

11.5 End of chapter questions

11.5.1 A company has decided to buy 50 laptop computers.

  (i) What features should they look for when deciding which laptops to buy?

  (ii) Discuss the relative advantages and disadvantages of using laptop computers compared to desktop computers.

11.5.2 (a) Name *two* household devices that use microprocessors.

  (b) For *each* named above, describe what functions the microprocessor controls.

11.5.3 A manufacturing company has decided to buy new input and output devices to allow it to carry out its day-to-day operations. The company manufactures parts which require welding, grinding and painting. There is also considerable office space where finance, management, research, design and customer relations/sales takes place.

  (a) Discuss the relative advantages and disadvantages of using dot matrix, inkjet and laser printers in the company. Part of your discussion should include where each printer type would be most suitable.

  (b) What input devices could be used in the company for:

    (i) Administration work

    (ii) Design and research work

    (iii) Video conferencing

    (iv) Security devices to allow entry to only certain personnel.

  (c) The company has several disabled workers. Discuss the specialist input and output devices which could help these workers interface with the computer systems.

11.5.4 (a) Describe the main differences between random access memory (RAM) and read only memory (ROM).

  (b) Various external, removable memory devices exist. Name a suitable device, giving a different example in each case, which could be used in the following applications. Give a reason for your choice in each case:

    (i) Storing multimedia files

    (ii) Storing music files

    (iii) Storing documents produced in a word processor

    (iv) Backing up files for security purposes

    (v) A security camera recording system that allows the security staff to record and playback at the same time.

11.5.5 (a) A music file is 40 Mbytes in size. Approximately, how much memory would the same music file need if it was stored in MP3 format?

(b) Why have CDs and DVDs taken over from floppy disks as the main secondary (memory) storage media on home computer systems?

11.5.6 A railway station management team has decided to introduce information kiosks to keep passengers up to date regarding train arrivals/departures and time tables. These kiosks will be unmanned and each kiosk will have six large TFT monitors.

(a) What input devices could be used at these information kiosks?

(b) What advantages do these kiosks give customers compared to manned information desks?

(c) What advantages does the system give to the management team?

(d) Apart from arrivals/departures and time tables, what other information could be made available to passengers at the railway station?

11.5.7 (a) Describe how LED technology is used in LCD flat screen monitors. What are the main benefits of using LED technology in this application?

(b) (i) Name the two types of technology used to 'spray' ink onto paper using inkjet printers.

(ii) Give one difference of each type of technology.

(c) (i) Explain the main differences in ink technology used by inkjet and laserjet printers.

(ii) Why are laserjet printers considered to be a potential health hazard when used in an office environment?

(d) Explain the role of buffers when carrying out a printing operation.

11.5.8 A CD contains 12 music files (songs). Each song requires 216 000 bytes of memory for each second of recording.

(a) (i) If each song lasts (on average) for 5 minutes 20 seconds, how much memory does each song use on the CD?

(ii) How much memory is used to store all 12 music files?

(b) It is possible to download this CD from an Internet music store. If the download speed offered by a service provider is: 56 megabytes/second, how long would it take to download all 12 music files?

(c) It was decided to store the CD in MP3 format. Assuming this gives 90 per cent reduction in the file size, how much memory would the 12 files occupy in the MP3 format?

11.5.9 (a) How are scanners used at airports to read passports?

(b) (i) How are barcodes used at the checkout of a supermarket?

(ii) Which other hardware devices are used at the supermarket checkout? Describe the use of each named device.

11.5.10 (a) What is the difference between lossy and lossless data compression?

(b) Describe how jpeg file technology is used to store photos in a format that generally retains the quality of the original photo but uses up less memory when the files are stored.

(c) Apart from memory requirements, give another advantage in storing files in the jpeg format.

(d) By using arrows, connect the memory/storage devices on the left to their correct descriptions shown on the right. Each description can be used only once.

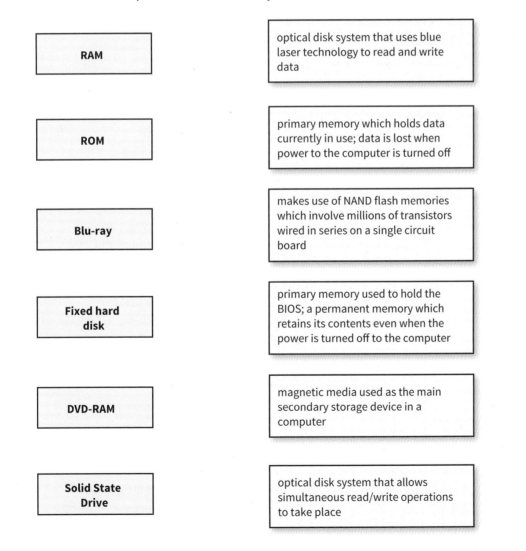

| RAM | | optical disk system that uses blue laser technology to read and write data |

| ROM | | primary memory which holds data currently in use; data is lost when power to the computer is turned off |

| Blu-ray | | makes use of NAND flash memories which involve millions of transistors wired in series on a single circuit board |

| Fixed hard disk | | primary memory used to hold the BIOS; a permanent memory which retains its contents even when the power is turned off to the computer |

| DVD-RAM | | magnetic media used as the main secondary storage device in a computer |

| Solid State Drive | | optical disk system that allows simultaneous read/write operations to take place |

12 Operating systems

Learning Summary

In this chapter you will learn about:
- *Operating systems*
- *Interrupts*
- *Batch processing*
- *Real time processing*
- *Computer architecture*
- *Fetch-Execute cycle*
- *Data transmission*

Many of the tasks carried out by computers are taken for granted. This is often down to a good operating system which automatically carries out many of the mundane tasks such as interrupt handling, user interface and so on. There are also specialist areas such as batch processing, real time processing and network systems. Computer architecture is an important part in the understanding of how computers work, together with the knowledge of how data is transmitted to and from a computer.

12.1 Operating systems

The *operating system (OS)* manages the basic tasks carried out by a computer, such as input from a keyboard, output to a printer, file management, security and device drivers. It provides a software platform which enables applications programs to run. On many computers, when it is powered up, the first program that runs is stored on a ROM chip. This program checks system hardware to make sure everything functions normally. The next thing to check is the CPU, the internal memory and basic input-output system (bios) for errors. If all proves to be acceptable, the *bios* activates the memory drives. When the hard drive is activated, the operating system is found and is loaded.

The operating system carries out a number of functions.

We have discussed the role of microprocessors in household devices. Many of these devices do not require an operating system (such as dish washer, refrigerator). The microprocessor has just one set of tasks to perform; the system expects simple inputs and they have simple, never-changing hardware functions to control. Thus, an operating system is not necessary, leading to lower costs at both development and manufacturing stages.

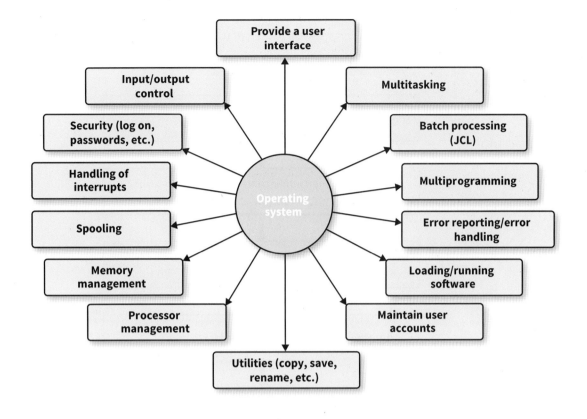

12.2 Interrupts

An *interrupt* is a signal sent from a device or from a running program to the processor; this causes the processor to stop what it is doing and service this interrupt signal. Interrupts can be caused by, for example:

- the printer needs more data to be sent to it
- errors, for example, printer has run out of paper or paper is jammed
- user interrupt, for example, user presses the <BREAK> key
- software error, for example, program tries to divide by zero.

Once the interrupt signal is received, the processor either carries on with what it was doing or stops to service the device/program that generated the interrupt.

Interrupts allow computers to *multi-task*, for example, printing a document whilst listening to some music from the computer library. If an interrupt is serviced, the state of the current task being run is saved; the processor goes to an *interrupt handler* and once the interrupt is fully serviced, the state of the interrupted task is reinstated and it resumes from where it left off.

Earlier in the book, the concept of a buffer was also introduced. The following sequence shows how interrupts and buffers are used when a stand-alone computer prints out a document which contains several pages.

data to be printed is sent to the (printer) **buffer** from the computer memory

the processor carries on with other tasks ....

.... while the (printer) **buffer** contents are emptied to the printer

when the (printer) buffer is empty, an **interrupt** is sent to the processor ....

.... from the printer, requesting more data to be sent

the current task is suspended whilst the **interrupt** is serviced

the **buffer** is refilled and the above sequence repeated until all the data has been sent to the printer

(since other interrupts may be received by the processor, all interrupts are given a **priority**)

> It is suggested that the reader carries out some research to find out how interrupt priorities work.

12.3 Batch processing

> Usually the work is done when computer resources are less busy (during the night).

In **batch processing**, a number of tasks called **jobs** are all collected together over a given period of time. These jobs are then loaded into a computer system (this is called a **job queue**) and processed all in one go, i.e. a **batch**. Once the job begins, it continues until it is finished or encounters an error. No user interaction is required once the job begins. Batch processing cannot be used where immediate action is required since file updating, for example, may not be completed for several hours (or days) later. Batch processing is often used in the following application areas:

– billing systems (gas, electricity, telephone, water, etc.)
– payroll systems
– processing of bank cheques.

Batch processing, for example; *electricity bills*

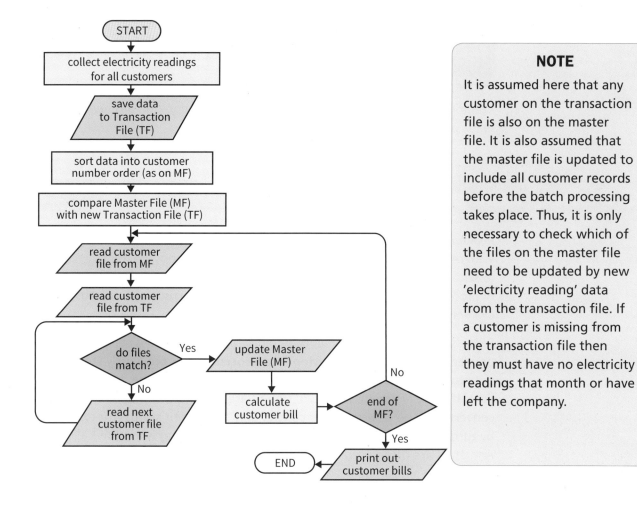

NOTE

It is assumed here that any customer on the transaction file is also on the master file. It is also assumed that the master file is updated to include all customer records before the batch processing takes place. Thus, it is only necessary to check which of the files on the master file need to be updated by new 'electricity reading' data from the transaction file. If a customer is missing from the transaction file then they must have no electricity readings that month or have left the company.

12.4   Real time transaction processing

Consider the following example:

- a customer calls a travel agent to book a seat on a flight
- using a computer terminal, the travel agent contacts the airline
- the customer's details (name, address, passport, date and time of flight, destination airport, etc.) are all input
- the airline's database is searched to match the customer requirements
- if seats are available, the customer is informed
- if the customer decides to go ahead with the booking, the seats are booked and the database updated immediately
- these seats on the flight are now flagged as 'UNAVAILABLE'.

To avoid double booking, the above application has to be done in *real time* and the databases have to be updated immediately. The response to any query also has to be immediate. This is an example of *real time transaction processing* which is very different to batch processing where responses and action to responses is not time critical.

> **Key Point** Any application which requires immediate response to a query and/or processing following the query must be done using real time transaction processing.

Examples include: booking theatre/cinema tickets, booking airline/train seats, obtaining money from an ATM, and so on.

12.5 Real time process control

Real time process control is very different to real time transaction processing. With real time process control, sensors and feedback loops are used (essentially, the output can influence the next input to the system). This type of processing does not involve updating databases or customer accounts, for example.

Sensors send data via an analogue to digital converter to a computer or microprocessor. The computer/microprocessor uses previously stored data to decide if any action needs to be taken based on the new sensor data. If some change is required, signals are sent via a digital to analogue converter to the devices under control and alters their status (for example, by turning on a heater if a temperature sensor reading is too low). Actuators are often used to open/close valves, switch on electric circuits, etc. This system can be used to continuously monitor or control some processes.

12.6 Computer architecture

The Von Neumann model

The *Von Neumann* model was first devised in 1945 as part of a report on the *stored program concept*. The following diagram shows the concept of the Von Neumann computer model.

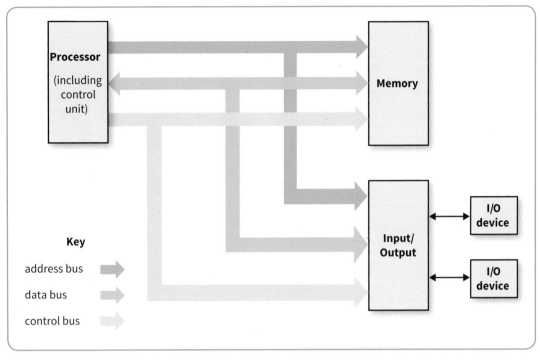

Von Neumann computer model

As can be seen in the figure above, information is moved around the system using connections known as a ***bus***. Three main types of bus are shown in the figure.

Address bus	– this carries signals relating to addresses between the processor and the memory; it is ***unidirectional*** (can carry signal in one direction only)
	– see later in this chapter for more information on addresses
Data bus	– this is used to exchange data between the processor, memory and input/output devices; it is ***bi-directional*** (can carry signals in both directions)
Control bus	– this carries signals relating to the control and coordination of activities within the computer (for example: the read and write functions).

However, the figure can be re-written to show more information about the actual main components in a typical computer system in the following manner.

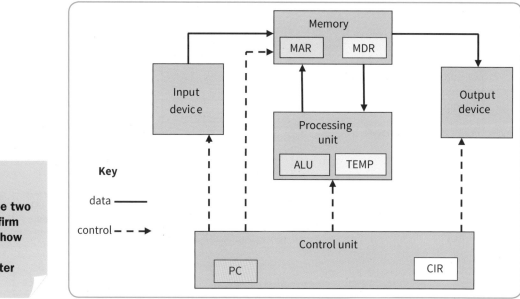

Main components in a computer system

We will now consider the five main components shown in the figure.

Memory

The computer memory is made up of partitions (much like a set of drawers). Each 'drawer' consists of an *address* and its *contents*. The example on the right uses 4 bits for each address and the contents are made up of 1 byte (8 bits). In reality, the address and its contents are usually much larger than this!! The address will uniquely identify every *location* in the memory (much like the address used to uniquely identify the location of a house in a particular city) and the contents will be the binary value stored in each location.

The figure on page 159 also shows that the memory is made up of items known as the **MAR (memory address register)** and the **MDR (memory data register)**. These work as follows:

- *to READ/LOAD data from a memory location called* L*:*
  - the address of location *L* to be read from is written into MAR
  - a 'read' signal is then sent to the computer memory
  - and the data is read from memory location *L* into MDR.

Thus, if data in memory location 0010 is to be read, 0010 is written into MAR and the data value at that location,11001100, is read into MDR.

- *to WRITE/STORE data into a location* L*:*
  - the data to be stored is written into the MDR
  - the address of location *L* is written into MAR
  - a 'write' signal is sent to the computer memory.

Thus, if data 11110001 is to be written into the memory location with address 1101, the data value 11110001 will first be written into MDR and then the address value 1101 will be written into MAR.

address	contents
0000	00110000
0001	01011001
0010	11001100
0011	00011000
1100	10001000
1101	11110001
1110	11000000
1111	00010001

It is left as an exercise to the reader to link the two figures – to confirm that they both show the same links between computer components.

Processing unit

The *processing unit* is made up of the *arithmetic and logic unit (ALU)* and *registers*. The ALU allows arithmetic (for example, add, and subtract) and logic (for example, AND, OR, NOT) operations to be carried out. Registers are temporary storage areas and also contain the results from the ALU.

Also refer to chapter 10 (binary systems) for more information about registers.

Input/Output devices

These are covered in great depth in chapter 11 and are the primary way of entering data into and getting information from computer systems. Input devices convert external data into a form the computer can understand and can then process (for example, keyboards and microphones). Output devices show the results of computer processing in a human readable form (for example, printers and monitors).

Control unit

The *control unit* controls the operation of the memory, processor and input/output devices. It contains the *current instruction register (CIR)* and the *program counter (PC)*. The CIR will contain the current instruction during processing. The PC contains the address of the next instruction to be executed.

Basically, the control unit reads an instruction from memory (the address of where the instruction is found is stored in the PC) and then interprets this instruction, generating signals to tell the other components in the computer what to do.

12.7 Fetch–execute cycle

Fetch

In the *fetch–execute cycle* the next instruction is *fetched* from the memory address currently stored in the program counter (PC) and is then stored in the current instruction register (CIR). The PC is then incremented so that the next instruction can be acted upon.

The decoder then interprets this instruction in the next part of the cycle.

Execute

The control unit (CU) passes the decoded information as a set of control signals to the appropriate components within the computer. This allows all necessary actions to be carried out.

For completeness, the following lists the actual stages that take place during the fetch–execute cycle showing the role of all the registers and buses in the process (the first five boxes are the fetch cycle and the last two boxes are the execute cycle).

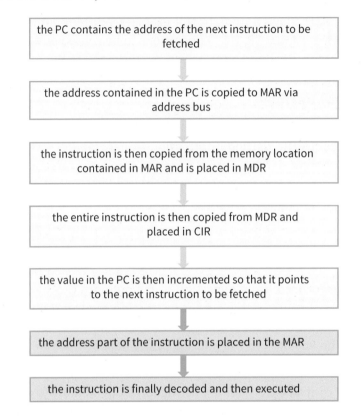

12.8   Data transmission

When data is transmitted between two machines, it can occur in a number of different ways. The transmission is characterised by:

- the *direction* of the data transmission (one way or two way transmission)
- the *method* of transmission (number of bits sent simultaneously)
- the *method of synchronisation* between sender and receiver.

Simplex, half-duplex and full-duplex connections

Simplex

Simplex data transmission allows data to flow *in one direction only*, i.e. from sender to receiver only. An example of this is when sending data from a computer to a printer.

Half-duplex

Half-duplex data transmission allows data to flow in both directions *but not at the same time*; data can be sent from sender to receiver and from receiver to sender but only one way at a time. An example of this would be a phone conversation where only one person speaks at a time.

Full-duplex

Full-duplex data transmission allows data to flow in **both directions simultaneously**. An example could be when using a broadband connection on a phone line.

Serial and Parallel data transmission

Parallel

Parallel data transmission refers to the transmission of several bits of data (often 1 byte at a time) **simultaneously** along a number of wires or channels.

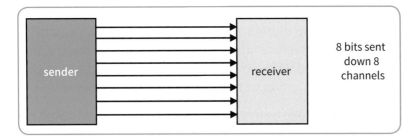

This method works well over short distances and is a much faster method of data transmission than serial. However, since the conductive wires are close to each other in the ribbon cables used for parallel transmission, interference can occur and degrade the signal quality.

An example of use of parallel data transmission is sending data from a computer to a printer.

Serial

Serial data transmission refers to data being transmitted **one bit at a time** over a single wire/channel.

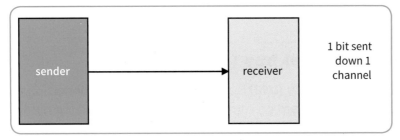

This method works well over long distances but has a slower transmission rate than parallel. However, cabling tends to be cheaper since fewer channels are required. Since a single wire is used, problems exist in how to synchronise the sender and receiver (i.e. the receiver cannot necessarily distinguish characters being sent because the bits are sent one after the other).

An example of serial data transmission is sending data from a computer to a modem for onward transmission over the telephone network.

Asynchronous and synchronous data transmission

Asynchronous

With *asynchronous* transmission, signals are sent in a previously agreed pattern of bits. The bits being sent are grouped together and consist of actual data and *control bits*. In other words, a *start bit* is sent at the beginning of the group of data and a *stop bit* is sent at the end of the group of data. This therefore informs the receiver where the transmitted group of bits starts and where it ends. Otherwise it would be impossible to distinguish when each group of bits is being received.

It is an inexpensive and effective form of serial transmission and is best suited to low speed connections such as keyboards and mouse.

Synchronous

Synchronous transmission is a data transfer method where a continuous stream of data is also accompanied by timing signals (generated by the internal electronic clock) to ensure sender and receiver are in step (i.e. synchronised with each other). With this method, the receiver counts the bits sent and then reassembles the bytes. It is essential that timing is maintained as there are no start and stop bits and no gaps (as in asynchronous transmission). Accuracy is dependent on the receiver keeping an accurate count of the bits as they come in.

It is faster than asynchronous transmission since fewer bits are sent and is therefore the choice for network communications links.

Universal serial bus (USB)

The *universal serial bus (USB)* is an asynchronous serial connection that has become the standard on computer systems and associated hardware. It consists of a four-wired shielded cable with two wires for power and earth and two wires for data transmission. When a device is plugged into a computer using one of the USB ports, the computer automatically detects the device due to a change in voltage level on the data signal wires. The appropriate *device driver* is then usually loaded up so that all the device features can be utilised and it also allows communication between device and CPU.

However, there are a number of benefits and drawbacks in using the USB standard.

Benefits	Drawbacks
Hardware devices are automatically detected and can be configured when first attached (loads up device driver)	Cable length is limited to 5 metres
USB connectors are shaped so that it is not possible to install devices incorrectly	Transmission speed is limited to 480 megabits/second (Mbps)
The USB standard is an 'open standard' and has considerable industry support	
USB connectivity supports many different data transmission speeds and data transfer types	USB support may not be available for very long when using older devices or earlier operating systems
The latest USB 2.0 standard is backward compatible with the older USB 1.1 standard	

Error checking following data transmission

The methods used to determine if any errors have occurred during the transmission of data are covered in chapter 10 of this book.

As mentioned earlier, USB connections make use of serial data transmission. They are often used to transfer data to a printer or to some external storage device.

Parallel data transmission is used in the internal circuitry of a computer or many other electronic devices. Since these devices are made up essentially of *integrated circuits* (ICs), where all the parts are linked using buses (see earlier), the method of data transmission is parallel. The transmission channels are usually 8-bit, 16-bit, 32-bit or 64-bit – the wider the channel then the faster the data transmission rate. An internal clock inside the device ensures that all of the transmitted bits arrive in sequence.

12.9 End of chapter questions

12.9.1 (a) Name **five** functions of a typical operating system.

(b) Explain why many microprocessor-controlled household devices do not have an operating system as part of their software.

12.9.2 Explain the difference between *real time transaction processing* and *real time process control*.

12.9.3 (a) Name the **three** types of *buses* used to connect up computer components according to the Von Neumann model.

(b) Name the **four** main components of a typical computer system according to the Von Neumann model.

address	contents
100000	0111 1110
100001	0110 1111
100010	1001 1000
100011	1111 0000
111000	
111001	
111010	
111011	

12.9.4 (a) What is meant by the two computer terms: **MAR** and **MDR**?

(b) Using the diagram on the right.

(i) if the **MAR** contained **100010** what would be contained in the **MDR** following a read signal sent to the memory?

(ii) if the **MDR** contained the value **1011 1010** and the **MAR** contained **111001**, show the change produced in the diagram on the right following a write signal being sent to memory.

(c) Name and describe **two** other registers.

12.9.5 Put the following stages in a typical *fetch–execute* cycle into their correct order. The first one has been done for you.

Description of stage	Order of carrying out each stage
Address contained in PC is copied to MAR via address bus	
Address part of instruction is placed in MAR	
Entire instruction is then copied from MBR and placed in CIR	
Instruction is finally decoded and then executed	
Instruction is then copied from memory location contained in MAR and is placed in MBR	
PC contains the address of the next instruction to be fetched	1
Value in the PC is then incremented so that it points to the next instruction to be fetched	

12.9.6 (a) What is meant by *parallel data being sent using simplex data transmission*?

(b) What is meant by *serial data being sent using half-duplex data transmission*?

12.9.7 (a) Describe the main differences between asynchronous and synchronous data transmission.

(b) (i) Give **two** benefits of using a USB to connect a device to a computer.

(ii) Give **two** drawbacks of using a USB to connect a device to a computer.

13.1 Practice paper 1

1 **Five** applications are shown on the left and **five** methods of automatic data capture on the right. Match **each** application to the correct method of data capture by drawing connecting arrows.

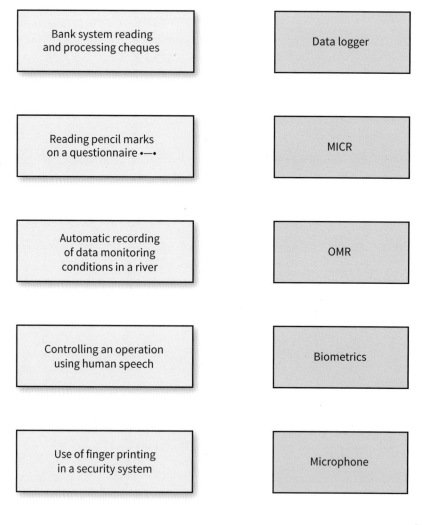

Bank system reading and processing cheques	Data logger
Reading pencil marks on a questionnaire •—•	MICR
Automatic recording of data monitoring conditions in a river	OMR
Controlling an operation using human speech	Biometrics
Use of finger printing in a security system	Microphone

[5]

2 A large tank has its acidity monitored and controlled by sensors and a microprocessor.

Acid can be added, as necessary, by controlling a valve and by switching on a stirrer.

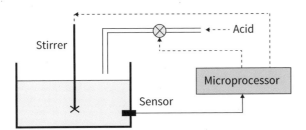

(a) Describe how sensors and the microprocessor are used to control the acidity level in the tank.

....

....

....

....

....

....

.... [4]

(b) Give **two** advantages of using microprocessor control of a process.

1 ....

....

2 ....

.... [2]

(c) In the above example, what is the difference between *monitoring* the tank conditions and *controlling* the tank conditions?

....

....

....

.... [2]

3 Describe how to guard against **each** of the following **five** security threats to Internet users:

phishing: ....

....

....

hacking: ....

....

....

viruses: ....

....

....

wardriving (tapping into WiFi): ....

....

....

fraud (reading credit card numbers): ....

....

.... [5]

4 Give a suitable application, with reasons for your choice, for **each** of the following types of printer. A different application should be given in each case:

laserjet printer

application: ....

....

reason for choice: ....

....

....

dot matrix printer

application: ....

....

reason for choice: ....

....

....

3D inkjet printer

application: ....

....

reason for choice: ....

....

.... [6]

5 Five computer terms are **described on the left** below and five computer terms are **named on the right** below.

Connect the correct description to the correct term by drawing arrows on the diagram below:

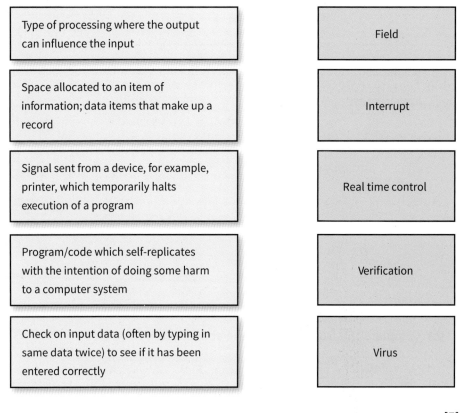

Type of processing where the output can influence the input	Field
Space allocated to an item of information; data items that make up a record	Interrupt
Signal sent from a device, for example, printer, which temporarily halts execution of a program	Real time control
Program/code which self-replicates with the intention of doing some harm to a computer system	Verification
Check on input data (often by typing in same data twice) to see if it has been entered correctly	Virus

[5]

6 A burglar system alarms (i.e. A = 1) according to the status of three inputs:

Input	Binary values	Conditions
W	1	intruder detected by window sensor
	0	no intruder detected by window sensor
D	1	intruder detected by door sensor
	0	no intruder detected by door sensor
F	1	fault condition identified
	0	no fault condition identified

The alarm, A, returns a value of 1 if:

either: intruder detected by window sensor **or** by door sensor **and** no fault condition identified

or: no intruder detected by window sensor **and** by door sensor **and** a fault condition is identified

(a) Draw the logic circuit for the above system, showing all your working:

working: ....

....

....

....

.... [2]

logic circuit:

[5]

(b) Complete the truth table for the above system:

W	D	F	A
0	0	0	
0	0	1	
0	1	0	
0	1	1	
1	0	0	
1	0	1	
1	1	0	
1	1	1	

[4]

7 A computer system is being used to display on a control panel the speed (in km/h) of a high speed train.

Each digit is represented by a 4-bit binary code. For example:

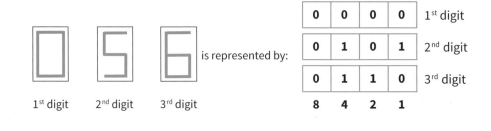

(a) What values must be in the 4-bit registers to represent the following speed shown on the speedometer?

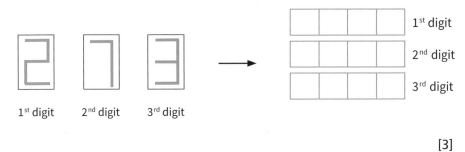

1st digit   2nd digit   3rd digit

[ ] [ ] [ ] [ ] 1st digit
[ ] [ ] [ ] [ ] 2nd digit
[ ] [ ] [ ] [ ] 3rd digit

[3]

(b) What is shown on the digital speedometer if the 4-bit registers contain the following values:

0	0	0	1	1st digit
0	1	0	0	2nd digit
1	0	0	1	3rd digit

1st digit   2nd digit   3rd digit

[3]

(c) What is the *theoretical* maximum speed which can be displayed?

.... [1]

(d) Give **one** advantage of showing speed in digital form rather than in analogue form.

....

.... [1]

8 (a) Convert the denary (base 10) number **202** into binary, and hex notation:

binary [ ][ ][ ][ ][ ][ ][ ][ ]

hex [ ][ ]   [2]

(b) (i) Perform the **AND** logical function on the two values A and B below:

A | 1 | 1 | 0 | 1 | 0 | 1 | 1 | 1 |

B | 1 | 0 | 0 | 1 | 1 | 1 | 1 | 1 |

A **AND** B [ ][ ][ ][ ][ ][ ][ ][ ]   [2]

(ii) What is the hexadecimal value of the above result?

[ ][ ]

9 **(a)** What is meant by *even parity*?

....

....

.... [1]

(b) The following seven bytes are transmitted together with a parity byte (even parity is being used). One of the bytes has been incorrectly transmitted since one of the bits is incorrect.

	parity bit	column 2	column 3	column 4	column 5	column 6	column 7	column 8
byte 1	1	1	0	1	1	1	0	1
byte 2	0	1	1	1	0	0	0	1
byte 3	1	0	0	1	1	1	1	0
byte 4	1	0	0	0	1	0	1	1
byte 5	0	0 ·	0	1	1	0	0	0
byte 6	1	1	1	1	1	1	0	0
byte 7	1	1	0	0	0	1	1	0
parity byte	1	0	0	1	1	0	0	1

(i) Identify the column and row of the bit which has been incorrectly transmitted:

column: ....

row: ....

[2]

(ii) Explain how you arrived at your answer to (i).

....

....

....

....

....

....

.... [3]

You should have written and tested a program to complete these three tasks before attempting Section A of this Paper.

Task 1. Input and store the names and times in minutes for 20 students who have run the school marathon race. Anyone taking more than 300 minutes is disqualified. You must store the names in a one-dimensional array and the times for each student in one-dimensional array. All the times must be validated on entry and any invalid times rejected. You may assume that the students' names are unique.

Task 2. Find the fastest and slowest times; calculate the average time for the whole class. Output the fastest, slowest and average times.

Task 3. Select the students with the three fastest times and output their name and times.

Your program must include appropriate prompts for the entry of data. Error messages and other output need to be clearly set out and understandable. All variables, constants and other identifiers should have meaningful names. Each task must be a separate part of the program and be fully tested.

Section A

1 (a) Declare the arrays to store the students' names and times in minutes.

....

.... [2]

(b) Using pseudocode or a flowchart, show the design of your algorithm to complete **Tasks 1 and 2.**

....

....

....

....

....

....

....

....

....

....

....

....

....

....

....

....

....

.... [7]

(c) Show **two** different sets of student data that you could use to check the validation used in Task 1. Explain why you chose each data set.

Set 1 ....

Reason for choice ....

....

....

Set 2 ....

Reason for choice ....

....

.... [4]

(d) (i) Explain how you select the students with the three fastest times **(Task 3)**, you may include pseudocode or program code to help illustrate your explanation.

....

....

....

....

....

....

....

....

....

....

....

.... [6]

(ii) How does your program work when there is more than one student with the same time?

....

....

.... [1]

Section B

2 A company offer back issues of football team annuals. The following data has to be typed into a computer screen page to order a back issue:

- 16-digit credit card number
- name of the person
- today's date in the form: dd/mm/yyyy
- price of the annual (in $)
- year of annual
- name of the football team.

(a) Name a validation check which could be used on some of the data items. Give a different validation check in each case.

name of person: ....

....

today's date: ....

....

price of annual: ....

....

year of annual: ....

.... [4]

(b) Describe how *check digits* are used as a method of validation.

....

....

....

....

....

....

.... [3]

3 Study the following flowchart very carefully:

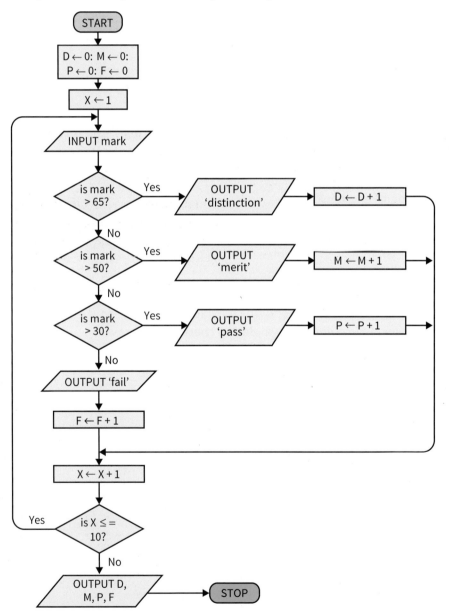

Complete the trace table for the following data set:

78, 51, 23, 60, 70, 50, 4, 80, 44, 39

X	mark	D	M	P	F	output

[6]

4 (a) Read the following section of code that inputs thirty (30) numbers, checks if they are positive or negative and then outputs the sum of the positive numbers.

```
1  counter = 0
2  repeat
3  read x
4     if x < 0 then total = total +1
5     counter = counter + 1
6     print total
7  until counter = 20
```

There are **three** errors in this code. Locate these errors and suggest a corrected piece of code.

1 ....

....

....

2 ....

....

....

3 ....

....

.... [3]

(b) The above code is an example of a high level language. High level languages can use a compiler or an interpreter. Explain the difference between a compiler and an interpreter.

....

....

....

....

.... [2]

5 The height of buildings and number of floors in buildings was being analysed.
Write an algorithm, using pseudocode or flowchart only, which:

- inputs the height and number of floors for 200 buildings
- outputs the average height of all the buildings
- outputs the number of buildings with more than 50 floors
- outputs the height of the tallest building.

....

....

....

....

....

....

....

....

....

....

....

....

....

....

....

....

.... [6]

6 A floor turtle can use the following instructions:

Instruction	Meaning of instruction
FORWARD *d*	move *d* cm forwards
BACKWARD *d*	move *d* cm backwards
LEFT *r*	turn left *r* degrees
RIGHT *r*	turn right *r* degrees
REPEAT *n*	repeat next set of instructions *n* times
ENDREPEAT	finish repeating instructions
PENUP	lift/raise the pen
PENDOWN	lower the pen

(NOTE: each square is 20 cm by 20 cm):

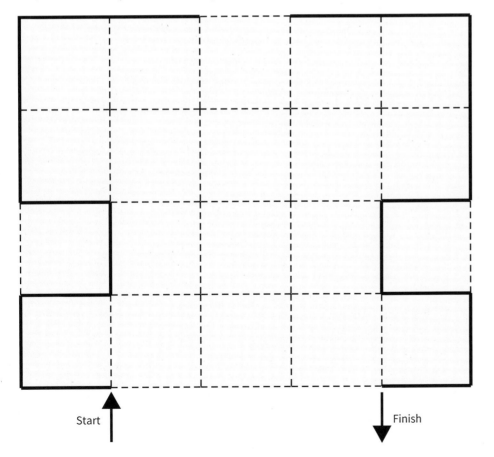

Start

Finish

Complete the following sequence of instructions to draw the above shape:

PENDOWN   ....
LEFT 90   ....
FORWARD 20   ....
....
....
....
....
....
....
....
....
....
....
....
....
....
....   [6]

Answers to questions

Chapter 2

2.5.1 (a) Monitoring a process:
  - Sensors send data
  - Data converted to digital data (using ADC)
  - Computer analyses/compares data
  - If outside the range (when compared to stored values) …
  - … it sends a signal to sound alarm or produce warning message on a screen.

  Controlling a process:
  - (*First* four lines are the same as above)
  - … it sends signals to actuators
  - Signals converted to analogue using DAC
  - Pumps/valves (etc.) are opened/closed (etc.) to alter the process conditions
  - The output affects the next input.

  (b) – Data gathered from temperature and pH sensors
  - Signals sent to ADC where they are converted to digital
  - Information is sent to the computer where it is compared to pre-set/stored values
  - If the temperature < 25°C, a signal is sent by the computer to switch on the heater (DAC is used to convert signal to analogue and actuators are used to switch on the heaters)
  - If the temperature > 30°C, a signal is sent by the computer to the motors to open the windows (again DAC and actuators used) and to switch off the heaters
  - If the temperature is between 25°C and 30°C, no action is taken
  - If the pH < 4, a signal is sent by the computer to open a valve to add alkaline water OR close the valve to stop adding acidic water (again DAC and actuators are used in the process)
  - If the pH > 5, a signal is sent by the computer to open valves to add acidic water (again use of DAC and actuators)
  - If the pH is between 4 and 5, no action is taken
  - In all cases, the output from the system will affect the next input to the system
  - Alarm is sounded if there is an error in the system
  - Monitoring and control continues until system turned off.

  (c) Light sensor – automatic doors in a hotel
  Acoustic sensor – picks up sounds, for example, a burglar alarm
  Infra red sensor – counting items every time the beam is broken.

2.5.2 (a) (i) Two problems – out of paint
  – component is missing
  – something is obstructing the paint spray gun.

  (ii) Use of sensors to detect out of paint, item is in the correct position, something is obstructing the spray gun, etc.
  Use of CCTV/cameras to show the status of the process (e.g. these can check paint surface of a car for imperfections).

  (b) Advantages:
  Can work in conditions hazardous/unpleasant to humans;
  They can work non-stop (no breaks);
  Less expensive in the long run (no wages required);
  More productive (takes less time to do a task than a human);
  More consistent (everything is always made to the same standard);
  Removes the need for humans to do boring/repetitive tasks;
  Less factory costs (can reduce heating, lighting levels, etc.).

  Disadvantages:
  Difficulty dealing with non-standard situations;
  Can lead to unemployment;
  Possible risk of deskilling;
  Production process can be more easily moved to 'less expensive' countries.

2.5.3 (a) – Pointing devices such as mouse
  - Touch screens

  (b) Command line interface: Direct communication with computer;
  Increases flexibility (GUI is very restricted);
  Graphical user interface: No need to understand how computers work;
  Much quicker/easier to find and open applications rather than have to type in a series of instructions.

2.5.4 (a)
- Sensors pick up proximity of objects
- Sensors pick up information from surroundings to make sure travelling Straight or can turn when path bends
- Data is sent to the computer
- This data is analysed by the computer
- Signals sent to wheels/motors to turn vehicle as needed (also use of DAC and actuators).

2.5.5 Capacitive

Benefits
- this is a medium cost technology
- screen visibility is good even in strong sunlight
- it permits multi-touch capability
- the screen is very durable; it takes a major impact to break the glass

Drawbacks
- allows only the use of bare fingers as the form of input; although the latest screens permit the use of a special stylus to be used

Infra red

Benefits
- both systems allow multi-touch capabilities
- the optical system allows the use of bare fingers, gloved fingers or stylus for input
- both systems have good screen durability; it takes a major impact to break the glass

Drawbacks
- it is a relatively expensive technology
- heat sensitive system only allows bare fingers to be used for input (gloved fingers or stylus don't work)
- both systems (optical and heat sensitive) have fairly good screen visibility in strong sunlight.

Resistive
- this makes use of an upper layer of polyester (a form of plastic) and a bottom layer of glass
- when the top polyester layer is touched, the top layer and bottom layer complete a circuit
- signals are then sent out which are interpreted by a microprocessor; the calculations determine the coordinates of where the screen was touched.

Benefits
- it is relatively inexpensive technology
- it is possible to use bare fingers, gloved fingers or stylus to carry out an input operation.

Drawbacks
- screen visibility is poor in strong sunlight
- it doesn't permit multi-touch capability
- the screen durability is only fair; it is vulnerable to scratches and the screen wears out through time

2.5.6
- sensors continually send data to the microprocessor
- if the output from the sensors is analogue, then the data is converted to digital, using an ADC, before it is sent to the microprocessor
- the microprocessor contains optimum temperature and acid/pH values (or they are stored on a storage device connected to the microprocessor)
- if the temperature reading is < 50°C then a signal is sent by the microprocessor to switch on the heater
- if the temperature > = 50°C then no action is taken
- if the pH reading is > 5, then a signal is sent to a valve to open and allow acid to enter chemical process
- if the pH < 5, then no action is taken
- the use of a DAC may be required depending on how the heater is switched on or valve is controlled the monitoring continues until the chemical process is completed

Chapter 3

3.5.1 (a) HTML
- Hypertext markup language
- Type of computer language
- All the text, graphics and design elements of a web page are tagged with codes that instruct a web browser how to display files on screen.

HTTP
- Hypertext transfer protocol
- Set of rules for transferring files on the web.

Search engine
- Way of finding information on websites
- User has to type in key words/queries

(b)
- Not all websites are accurate (anybody can set up a website)
- It is possible to access 'unwanted' or 'dangerous' websites and controls are needed to prevent access to certain sites
- The number of results (called *hits*) from a search engine could be massive; there is a need to narrow down the search using AND (+), OR or quotes (" "); for example:
- *type in CIE and the search engine returns ~ 46 million hits*
- *type in CIE+sample papers and the search engine returns ~56000 hits*
- *type in CIE+sample papers+Geography and the search engine returns ~7000 hits.*

3.5.2 (a) Features of dial up:
- This offers a fairly slow data transfer rate (typically ~ 60 kbps)
- There is a need to dial one of the numbers supplied by the ISP every time you want to connect to the Internet
- Because of the above, dial up isn't on all the time.
- The ISP contracts are usually for a number of hours per month and if this is exceeded additional charges are incurred.
- Another drawback is that the phone line is tied up while the user is accessing the Internet.

Features of broadband:
- This has a much faster data transfer rate (> 50 000 kbps).
- There is often an upper limit on the monthly download/upload file size (typically 20 Gbyte); this is not usually a problem unless the user frequently downloads music or film files
- It has the advantage of <u>always</u> being on but it doesn't tie up the phone line (i.e. phone calls can still be made even when the Internet is being accessed)
- Allows systems such as VoIP, on-line chatting in real time, C2C (webcam to webcam) to take place effectively.

(b) 80 tracks = 80 x 3.8
= 304 Mbyte
64 megabits/second = 8 Mbyte/second
thus time to download 80 tracks
= 304/8
= 38 seconds

(c) (i) 50 photos = 50 x 2
= 100 Mbyte
24 megabits/second = 3 Mbyte/second
thus time to upload 50 photos = 100/3
= 33 seconds

(ii) These sites are designed to promote the building of online communities who in general share the same interests and activities. They are aimed primarily at young people who can then share photos, videos, music, favourite foods and so on. They are usually free of charge and allow the interaction of people. Users can add friends, post messages to each other ('write on my wall') and update their personal profiles to notify friends about their likes and personal information. These sites are expanding quickly and there is some recent concern about their safety and security. However, they do allow easy interaction between like-minded people from different parts of the world which is a very positive move forward.

(iii) *Tagging* is a type of ***bookmarking*** where a user *tags* a web page or photograph (or whatever the users wishes) using some text to describe its contents. Anyone can view the web page or photographs corresponding to the tags. Suppose you have taken a photograph of your new car in 2010 showing Ipanema Beach in the background. Which folder do you place your photograph so you can easily find it again in 2 or 3 years' time? My cars? My 2010 photos? My favourite beaches? ...... or in all three (which then becomes a big waste of memory!). Tagging helps you out of this dilemma. It is now possible to tag the photograph with key words such as: *my cars, Ipanema Beach, 2010*. So when you (or a friend) come to find this photo 2 or 3 years later, you don't have to remember where you stored it. Simply search on the tag and all the matching photos will be displayed.

(d) This is data sent in a compressed form over the Internet and is displayed in real time on the user's computer. The downloaded data is sent to a ***buffer***; it isn't saved on the user's computer and needs to be ***streamed*** every time the video or audio file is to be accessed.

3.5.3 **Digital media web sites**: These websites allow users to ***upload*** video files and other multimedia files for other users to access as required.
The video files are stored on the ***server*** and allow either free access to anyone or some form of code is required before the videos can be viewed.
Since most users don't have unlimited web space, this type of website is becoming increasingly popular as a way of storing/archiving a number of videos.
Podcasts: are essentially a series of media files (audio and video) that are released at regular intervals and downloaded to a user's computer. Because of the method of delivery, this is a different way of accessing media files.
All the media files are stored and maintained centrally and the listener or viewer simply employs the appropriate application software to access these files, check for updates and download new files in the given series. Thus, it is possible to automatically download each episode/track of your favourite programme or artist as soon as it is made available.

3.5.4 (a) As a safeguard, users of chat rooms are warned about their language and use of the facility. It is important to prevent abuse, hassling of other members. etc. and there is a code of conduct which, if breached, would lead to a user being blocked from taking part in the future.

(b) ***Chat rooms*** use ***instant messaging (IM)*** to allow communication in real time. A user registers with a chat room and chooses a user name and password. When they wish to enter the chat room they log in with the user name and password.

Once they have entered the chat room, a list of people currently online will be alerted to them joining in. To chat, the user types into a text box and may sometimes use *emoticons*.

The message becomes immediately visible to all those on line. It is possible to enter a chat room to read messages only and not contribute – this is known as *lurking.*

(C) *Instant messaging (IM)* is sending real time messages to another Internet user. It is similar to chat rooms but is generally on a one-to-one basis and is therefore more private. Instant messaging is also a faster method of communication than using emails since it is in real time.

3.5.5 **(a)** **True:** information is sent straight to the user's computer and there is no need to save it first on the website server; the data is actually streamed live (i.e. in real time);

On-demand: the files are first saved on a hard disk on the web server and played back to the user when they are requested.

(b) Buffering is an important component here to enable continuous playback to an acceptable standard. The main advantage is there is no need to store media files and it is possible to always download the latest version from the central web host.

(C) There is a need to have media player software on the user's computer that uncompressed the data and is then sent to a buffer before being played back on a monitor or through speakers.

However, if the buffering is slow or the broadband connection is slow, there will be delays in the playback which can be very annoying. Many webcams also use this method to send video data over the network.

3.5.6 **(a)** Viruses, security issues, scamming, fraud, pornographic website.
- Intranets are safer since there is less chance of external hacking or viruses.
- It is possible to have more control, for example, it is easier to filter out websites that you don't want your work force to access.
- Companies can make sure that the information available to its employees is specific to their company needs.
- If there is a need to send out 'sensitive' information (e.g. security risk and data which could give competitors an advantage) it is easier to ensure that this information remains within the company.

(b) **Advantages:**
- Intranets are safer since there is less chance of external hacking or viruses.
- It is possible to have more control, for example, it is easier to filter out websites that you don't want your work force to access.

- Companies can make sure that the information available to its employees is specific to their company needs.
- If there is a need to send out 'sensitive' information (e.g. security risk and data which could give competitors an advantage) it is easier to ensure that this information remains within the company.

3.5.7 Web browsers, ISP, VoIP software/communications.

Chapter 4

4.9.1 **(a)** The private key is only known to the user's computer, while the public key is given by the user's computer to any other computer that wants to communicate securely with it. To decode an encrypted message, a computer must have the public key and the private key.

The sending computer encrypts the message with a symmetric key, then encrypts the symmetric key with the public key of the receiving computer. The receiving computer uses its private key to decode the symmetric key and then uses the symmetric key to decode the message.

(b) **List of stages:**
- The web browser attempts to connect to a website which is secured with SSL
- The web browser requests the web server to identify itself
- The web server sends the web browser a copy of its SSL certificate
- The web browser checks whether the SSL certificate is authentic/trustworthy; if it checks out as OK then the web browser sends a message back to the web server
- The web server will then send back some form of acknowledgement to allow the SSL encrypted session to begin
- The encrypted data is then shared securely between the web browser and the web server.

(c) *Passwords* – user name and password; when these are entered, they are checked against a secure file to confirm an authorised person has 'logged in' to the system – if either user name or password are incorrect, access is denied

Pass cards – pass cards contain a magnetic stripe (which contains security information) and/or an embedded chip (which often contains a PIN)

Digital signatures – digital signatures are based on public key encryption (which use a private key and a public key)

Biometrics – biometrics are a recent introduction; they rely on the unique properties of certain aspects of the human physiology:
- fingerprint scans
- retina scans

- face scan
- voice identification.

4.9.2 (a) List of features:

- Examine all the traffic routed between the private network and public network ....
- .... and check whether the traffic meets certain criteria
- If the criteria fails, the firewall will block the traffic
- It filters inbound and outbound traffic
- It can be used to log all attempts to enter a private network and warn of such attempts
- Can prevent access to undesirable websites or websites which pose a security risk
- It helps to prevent malware/viruses getting into computers on the private network
- It keeps a list of undesirable websites or IP addresses
- It keeps a list of acceptable websites/IP addresses
- It can reduce the risk of hacking from outside the private network
- It allows a user to accept or reject software trying to be downloaded from the Internet by software already installed on the user's computer.

(b) List of features:

- Proxy servers allow filtering of Internet traffic and can block access to certain websites
- Proxy servers help to speed up the access of information from web servers by using a cache; the website home page is saved on the proxy server cache (part of its memory area) after it is accessed for the first time – the next time the user wants to visit the same website, it is now accessed from the proxy server cache rather than from the remote web server; thus giving faster access
- Proxy servers help to keep a user's IP address anonymous thus improving Internet security
- Some proxy servers can act as a firewall improving security from, for example, hacking.

(c) An http cookie is a packet of information sent by a web server to a web browser and then sent back by the web browser to the web server every time it accesses it. Cookies are used to authenticate the user (e.g. messages such as: 'Welcome Nicolae. If you are not Nicolae please log out' appear each time the website is accessed by the user). Cookies also carry out user tracking and maintain user preferences (e.g. when visiting a music website, a user's music choice will be known as soon as they log on).

Cookies are not programs but are simply pieces of data and are unable to perform any operations on their own. They cannot erase or read data on the user's computer and only allow detection of web pages viewed by the user on a particular web site. Although this information is used to form an anonymous profile of the user, and don't contain personal data such as name and address, they have been the subject of some privacy concerns lately. For this reason, they have been included here in the security issues section of the textbook.

Nonetheless, cookies have been the subject of many misconceptions over the years. For example, none of the following are actually true:

- Cookies are like viruses and can do harm to data stored on a computer
- Cookies are a form of spyware/key logging software and can access and transmit personal data when typed on a computer keyboard
- Cookies generate website pop ups/pop unders
- Cookies are a form of spam.

4.9.3 (a) Hacking:

- Use *firewalls* (these provide a log of incoming and outgoing traffic and can essentially prevent malicious access to a user's computer or block access to unwanted Internet sites).
- Use robust passwords and user ids.
- Use of encryption (this doesn't stop illegal access to data but makes the intercepted data unreadable).
- Anti-hacking software is also available to help prevent hacking.

Viruses:

- Install and regularly use up-to-date *anti-virus software* (which detects and removes the virus or quarantines any files which have been infected).
- Do not use software from unknown sources (e.g. from the Internet and CDs).
- Take care when opening attachments from 'unknown' email addresses.

Phishing:

- Many ISPs can filter out these phishing emails, but users should always be aware of the risk and exercise caution when opening emails.

Pharming:

- Certain anti-spyware software can identify and remove pharming code.
- The user should always be alert and look out for 'clues' that they are being re-directed to another site.

War driving:

- Use of WEP encryption.
- Use of passwords.
- Use of firewalls.

Spyware:

- Certain anti-spyware software can identify and remove this type of code/software.
- The user should always be alert and look out for 'clues' that they are being monitored in this way.

Shoulder surfing:

- The user is advised to 'shield' the keyboard whilst they are typing a PIN into it, for example.

(b) (i) and (ii)

*Cookie*s are small files sent to a user's computer when they visit certain websites. They store information about the user which is accessed every time they visit the website.

For example, every time the user logs on to a website they may see a message such as '*Welcome back, Dmitry*'; or '*If you are not Dmitry Serdyuk then .....*' This allows a user's preferences to be recognised, for example, if a use often buys designer clothes, *pop-ups* (adverts) and pop-unders related to designer clothes companies will appear on the user's screen each time they visit the website. They are not malicious or harmful and are simply a way of letting the website know who you are. But they can 'clog' up a computer which through time will manifest itself as a slowing down of computer performance.

4.9.4 (i), (ii) and (iii)

All of the answers in question 4.9.3 could lead to data loss/ corruption and constitute illegal access. However, there are other factors which could lead to data loss or corruption and there are certain measures which can be taken to prevent or minimize these factors:

Accidental damage: use backups in case data is lost or corrupted; use passwords and user ids to restrict who has access to the data in the first place.

Hardware faults: hard disk (head) crash guarded against by using backup files; use of UPS (uninterruptable power supply) in case of power loss; use of parallel systems.

Software faults: use backups in case data is lost or corrupted by software failure.

Incorrect computer operation: correct training of the work force which is reinforced on a regular basis; keep backups of files just in case.

4.9.5 (a) *Wardriving* is the act of locating and using *WiFi (wireless Internet connection)* connections illegally; it usually involves driving round an area in a car to look for WiFi signals. This requires a computer, wireless net card (set to intercept and read network data packets) and an antenna which can pick up the signals. But, in general, tapping into a WiFi signal.

(b) Use of WEP encryption; use of passwords; use of firewall.

4.9.6

Description	Security risk	
	Yes	No
spyware	✓	
virus	✓	
cookie		✗
phishing	✓	
spam		✗
pharming	✓	
RSI		✗

4.9.7 (i) Encryption scrambles the data, therefore doesn't prevent access to files, it just makes them unreadable if illegally accessed.

(ii) DPA simply sets out the rules to protect data, but still can't prevent hacking or remove the risk of viruses; the act indicates that data security is a necessary requirement together with protecting the integrity of the data but illegal acts can't be prevented by an act on its own.

(iii) Spyware monitors actual key presses on a keyboard; looking at a PIN as it is being entered at an ATM is shoulder surfing and isn't a method of directly recording key presses as would happen with spyware.

(iv) The virus may be attached to the file itself; hence, backing up the files would not be an effective way of recovering from a virus since using the backed up files may simply reintroduce the virus to the system.

(v) Call centres tend to save companies' money since the workforce in the call centre countries tend to be less expensive to hire.

4.9.8 (a) Encryption is used in many cases to protect against the effects of illegal access to data (i.e. to prevent the hacker from understanding the data that has been intercepted).

However, many banks, for example, go one stage further when operating online banking. They encrypt all data but also use some of the following:

1 Use of user codes (this is often an 8-digit or 10-digit code unique to a user):

Please type in your user code:

2 Input some of the characters from a PIN and some of the characters from a password. This method prevents a hacker finding out the password/PIN, since each time a user logs onto the bank they will be asked to key in different characters; for example, in the example below, the user is asked to type in the 3rd, 4th and 1st characters from their PIN and the 2nd, 5th and 9th characters from their password:

Please type in the following characters from your PIN:

3rd

4th

1st

Please type in the following characters from your password:

2nd

5th

9th

3 Alternatively, the user might be asked, for example, to key in the 2nd, 5th and 9th characters from their password using drop down boxes. This method is a further attempt to stop spyware picking up key presses (since the user clicks on

the characters from the drop down boxes) and prevent the password characters becoming known to the spyware originator.

Please give the last four digits of your debit card:

> **2nd character**
>
> **5th character**
>
> **9th character**

'You were last logged in on 5th August, 2011. Is this correct?'

This is an additional check to ensure that only the official customer has tried to log on to the user account. If the customer had not logged in on the date supplied then this would indicate a potential security breach.

4 The user might also be asked to confirm some 'memorable' piece of information (such as mother's maiden name, user's mobile phone number).

5 Finally, many companies send out card readers which need to be used every time the customer wants to access their account on line:

Please insert your card into the card reader and enter your PIN.

Then key in the 8-digit code shown on your card reader:

The bank's computer will then check that this 8-digit code matches with the 8-digit code produced by the algorithm stored in its memory and will only allow access if they agree.

(b) They inform their customers that they will NEVER contact them about their account using the email system; any email received querying their account will come from some unauthorised source and should be treated with caution.

(c) – Debit/credit card placed in card reader
– Amount to be paid is keyed in
– Chip on card is accessed
– Card validity is checked (i.e. expiry date, is card stolen)
– A check is made on whether sufficient funds are available
– Customer is requested to key in PIN
– Keyed in PIN is then checked against PIN stored on chip
– If the card is valid and the PIN is OK .....
– ..... then the transaction is authorised
– Authorisation code sent to restaurant
– Amount of money for the meal is deducted from the customer's account
– Same amount is debited to restaurant account
– Receipt is produced as proof of purchase.

Chapter 5

5.6.1
```
PENDOWN
FORWARD 20
LEFT 90
FORWARD 20
RIGHT 135
FORWARD 20
PENUP
RIGHT 45
FORWARD 20
PENDOWN
RIGHT 90
FORWARD 20
RIGHT 135
FORWARD 20
LEFT 90
FORWARD 20
PENUP
```

5.6.2
```
PENDOWN
FORWARD 10
LEFT 90
REPEAT 3
FORWARD 20
RIGHT 90
ENDREPEAT
RIGHT/LEFT 180
PENUP
FORWARD 10
PENDOWN
LEFT 90
FORWARD 20
RIGHT 90
FORWARD 10
RIGHT 90
FORWARD 60
RIGHT 90
FORWARD 10
RIGHT 90
FORWARD 20
LEFT 90
PENUP
FORWARD 10
PENDOWN
LEFT 90
REPEAT 3
FORWARD 20
RIGHT 90
ENDREPEAT
LEFT 180
FORWARD 10
PENUP
```

5.6.3
```
var value : integer;
readln (value);
```

```
if value = 0 then write ('zero')
      else if value = 1 then write ('one')
            else if value = 2 then write ('two')
                  else write ('?');
   case value of
      0 : write ('zero');
      1 : write ('one');
      2 : write ('two');
      else write ('?')
   end;
input 0, zerozero
input 1, oneone
input 2 two,two
input 3 ??
input 4 ??
```

5.6.4

For loop
```
   Over20:=0;
   for count := 1 to 10 do
      begin
         readln (number);
         if number > 20 then over20 := over20 + 1
      end;
   writeln (over20 ' numbers were over 20');
while loop
   Over20 := 0;
   Count := 0;
   while count < 10 do
      begin
         readln (number);
         if number > 20 then over20 := over20 + 1;
         count := count + 1
      end;
   writeln (over20 ' numbers were over 20');
while loop
   Over20 := 0;
   Count := 0;
   while count < 10 do
      begin
         readln (number);
         if number > 20 then over20 := over20 + 1;
         count := count + 1
      end;
   writeln (over20 ' numbers were over 20');
repeat loop
   Over20 := 0;
   Count := 0;
   repeat
      begin
         readln (number);
         if number > 20 then over20 := over20 + 1;
         count := count + 1
      end
```

```
   until count = 10;
   writeln (over20 ' numbers were over 20');
```
A for loop should be chosen as the number of repetitions is known.

5.6.5

```
var array studentmark[1..20] of integer;
var total, highestmark, lowestmark, index : integer;
var average : real;
highestmark := 0;
lowestmark := 60;
total := 0;
for index := 1 to 20 do
   begin
      write ('Enter student mark ');
      readln (studentmark[index]);
      while (studentmark[index] < 0) or
                  (studentmark[index] > 60)
         begin
            write ('Enter student mark ');
            readln (studentmark[index]);
         end;
      if studentmark[index] > highestmark
         then highestmark := studentmark[index];
      if studentmark[index] < lowestmark
         then lowestmark := student 60ark[index];
      total := total + studentmark[index]
   end;
average:= total/20;
writeln ('Average is ', average);
writeln ('Highest mark is is ', highestmark);
writeln ('Lowest mark is ', lowestmark);
```

5.6.6

```
var name : string;
var age : integer;
var gender : char;
var count : integer;
const male = 'M';
const female = 'F';
write ('Enter your name ');
readln (name);
count := 0;
repeat
   begin
      write ('Enter your age ');
      readln (age);
      count := count + 1
   end
until ((age > 17) and (age < 101)) or (count = 3);
count := 0;
repeat
   begin
      write ('Enter your gender ');
      readln (gender);
```

```
        count := count + 1
    end
until (gender = male) or (gender = female)
                    or (count = 3);
```

5.6.7

```
var array week[1..7] of string;
var array rainfall [1..7] of real;
var array sunshine [1..7] of real;
var totalrainfall, totalsunshine : real;
var day : integer;
week[1] := 'Sunday';
week[2] := 'Monday';
week[3] := 'Tuesday';
week[4] := 'Wednesday';
week[5] := 'Thursday';
week[6] := 'Friday';
week[7]:= 'Saturday';
for day := 1 to 7 do
    begin
        write ('Enter hours of sunshine for ', week[day]);
        readln (sunshine[day]);
        totalsunshine := totalsunshine + sunshine[day];
        write ('Enter cms of rainfall for ', week[day]);
        readln (rainfall[day]);
        totalrainfall := totalrainfall + rainfall[day]
    end;
writeln ('Total sunshine for week is ', totalsunshine);
writeln ('Total rainfall for week is ', totalrainfall);
for day := 1 to 7 do
    begin
        if rainfall[day] = 0 then
            writeln ('no rainfall on ', week[day])
    end;
```

5.6.8

```
var discount1, discount2, cost : real;
var noplayers, nohours : integer;
readln (noplayers, nohours);
cost := noplayers * nohours * 5;
if noplayers >=3 then discount1 = cost * 0.25;
if nohours > 3 then discount2 = cost * 0.1;
cost = cost – discount1 – discount2;
writeln (cost);
```

Extension hint:

Assume that a file contains all members, so the algorithm will need player to input name and then check if it's on the file. Also input the PIN as four separate digits and check each digit in turn. If the name and PIN match, the formula in the third line changes to **noplayers * nohours * 4**

5.6.9 **(a) (i)** 8   **(ii)** 6

  (b) freezer id

(c) C, E, F, G, H

(d)

Field:	freezer id	lowest temp (C)	capacity (m3)
Table:	FREEZER FEATURES	FREEZER FEATURES	FREEZER FEATURES
Sort:			
Show:	☑	☐	☐
Criteria:		< -25	> 0.24
or:			

5.6.10 **(a)** 9

  (b) ref no

  (c) 2, 4, 5, 9

  (d)

Field:	ref no	km to airport	weekend tariff ($)	no of rooms
Table:	HOTELS	HOTELS	HOTELS	HOTELS
Sort:				
Show:	☑	☐	☐	☐
Criteria:			< 100	> 50
or:		< 10		

  (e)

Field:	ref no	weekend tariff ($)
Table:	HOTELS	HOTELS
Sort:		Ascending
Show:	☑	☐
Criteria:		
or:		

5.6.11 **(a)** Finance

  (b) M A J I D M F P G E R M A N Y 0 9

  (c) Fewer typing errors;
     Faster to type in the data;
     Uses less memory to store data.

  (d) It would be necessary to change/update the data every year.
     It would be better to use date person joined the company.

  (e) none of the fields can be guaranteed to be unique.

  (f) Staff Id, alphanumeric 6 characters, each member of staff could be given a unique identification code.

Chapter 6

6.5.1

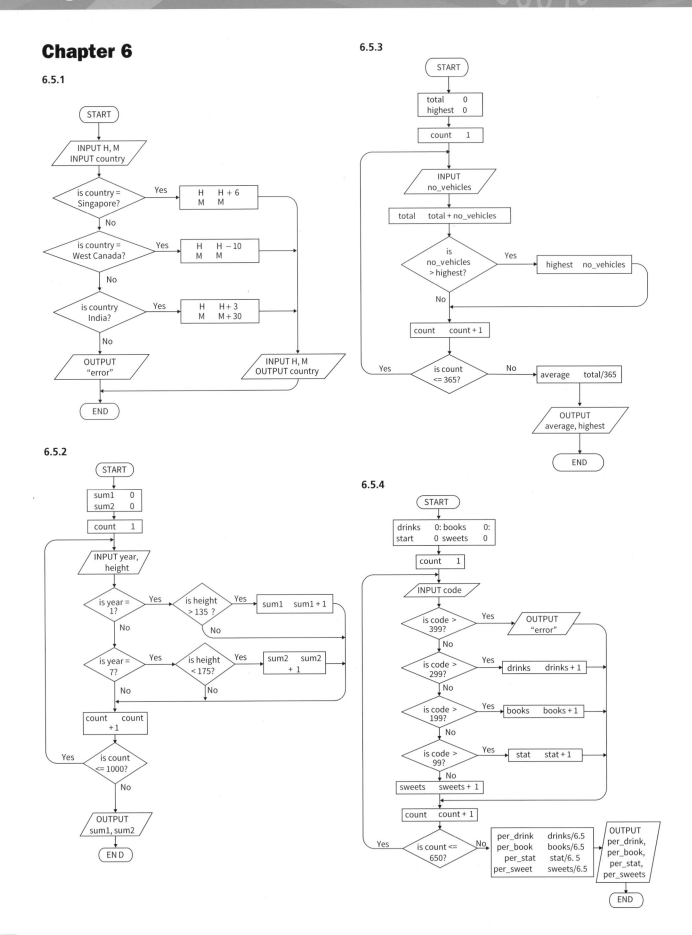

6.5.2

6.5.3

6.5.4

6.5.5

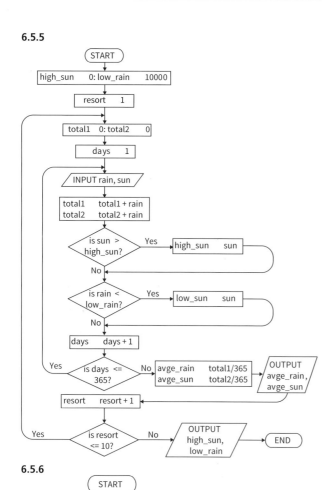

6.5.6

6.5.7

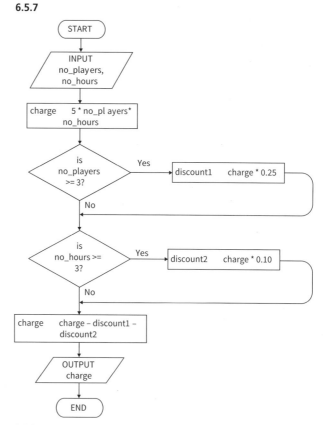

6.5.8

number	count	temp	OUTPUT
52	0	52	
	1	42	
	2	32	
	3	22	
	4	12	
	5	2	2, 52
−20	0	−20	error
3	0	3	
	1	−7	1, 3

6.5.9

sunny	wet	foggy	weather	OUTPUT
0	0	0		
1			sunny	
2			sunny	
	1		wet	
		1	foggy	
3			sunny	
	2		wet	
4			sunny	
	3		wet	
		2	foggy	
5			sunny	
			last	5, 3, 2

6.5.10

total1	total2	X	Y	count	temp	avge1	avge2	OUTPUT
0	0	0	0	1				
	24		1	2	24			
16		1		3	16			
	55		2	4	31			
36		2		5	20			
	83		3	6	28			
	104		4	7	21			
54		3		8	18			
70		4		9	16			
	129		5	10	25			
	154		6	11	25	17.5	25.7	17.5, 25.7

6.5.11

C	total	X	number	OUTPUT
1	0	0	40	
	40	1		
	4			
	0.4			40, 1
2	0	0	−5	
	−5			
	−0.5			−5, 0
3	0	0	3400	
	3400	1		
	340	2		
	34	3		
	3.4			
	0.34			3400, 3
4	0	0	800000	
	800000	1		
	80000	2		
	8000	3		
	800	4		
	80	5		
	8			
	0.8			800000, 5
5				

Chapter 7

7.3.1 line 3 – The algorithm inputs 5001 numbers
– The loop should be changed to: **for** x ← 1 **to** 4999
line 5 – The action taken after checking for the largest positive number is incorrect
– The statement should change to: pos ← number
line 6 – The action taken after checking for the largest negative number is incorrect
– The statement should change to: neg ← number
line 7 – The statement: x ← x +1 is not required when using **for .. to** loops
– Line 7 should be removed altogether

7.3.2 line 3 – No_ppl > 4 is incorrect (question referred to 3 or more)
– The statement should change to:
if no_ppl >= 3 ......
line 3 – The discount is incorrect, i.e. cost ← cost * 0.10 (this is equivalent to a 90% discount)
– The statement should change to: cost ← cost * 0.90
line 4 – Loop starts at 0 which is incorrect
– The statement should change to:
for x ← 1 **to** no_ppl

7.3.3 line 1 – Count is set to 0; this is incorrect
– Statement should change to: count ← 1
line 2 – Initialisation is set to 1 which is incorrect
– Statement should be changed to:
total_one ← 0: total_two ← 0
line 4 – Required to count numbers 1000 or over; the present statement ignores the number when it is equal to 1000
– Change statement to: **if** number >= 1000 ...
line 6 – Input is in the wrong place
– The input should come before the two **if** statements

7.3.4 10 **input** H, M, country$
20 **if** country$ = 'Singapore' **then** H ← H + 6
30 **else if** country$ = 'Western Canada' **then** H ← H – 10
40 **else if** country$ = 'India' **then** H ← H + 3: M ← M + 30
50 **else print** 'error'
60 **print** country$, H, M
extension question (add the following lines, for example):
55 **if** H > 23 **then** H ← H – 24: **print** 'next day'
56 **if** H < 0 **then** H ← H + 24: **print** 'previous day'
57 **if** M > 59 **then** M ← M – 60: H ← H + 1

7.3.5 10 total1 ← 0: total2 ← 0
20 **for** x ← 1 **to** 1000
30 **input** year, height
40 **if** year = 1 **and** height >= 135 **then** total1 ← total1 + 1
50 **else if** year = 7 **and** height < 175 **then** total2 ← total2 + 1
60 **next** x
70 **print** 'Year 1', total1, 'Year 7', total2

7.3.6 10 total ← 0: height ← 0
20 **for** x ← 1 **to** 365
30 **input** no_vehicles
40 total ← total + no_vehicles
50 **if** no_vehicles > highest **then** highest ← no_vehicles
60 **next** x
70 average ← total/365
80 **print** average, highest

7.3.7 In this example we could use the *case* statement instead of the way it has been done in lines 40 to 70. The method used in example 4 in the text book has not been used here since the sweets codes start at 000 and end

with 099 which means it would be impossible or difficult to do the same type of mathematical manipulation. In this method, we have split the code into three digits a, b, c and a check is made on the value of a.

```
10   sweets ← 0: stat ← 0: books ← 0: drinks ← 0
20   for x ← 1 to 650
30      input a, b, c
40      if a = 0 then sweets ← sweets + 1
50         else if a = 1 then stat ← stat + 1
60            else if a = 2 then books ← books + 1
70               else if a = 3 then drinks ← drinks + 1
80                  else print 'error'
90   next x
100  percent1 ← (sweets * 100)/650
110  percent2 ← (stat * 100)/650
120  percent3 ← (books * 100)/650
130  percent4 ← (drinks * 100)/650
140  print percent1, percent2, percent3, percent4
```

7.3.8
```
10   highest ← 0: lowest ← 10 000
20   for x ← 1 to 10
30      total1 ← 0: total2 ← 0
40      for year ← 1 to 365
50         input rain, sun
60         total1 ← total1 + rain
70         total2 ← total2 + sun
80         if sun > highest then highest ← sun
90            else if rain < lowest then lowest ← rain
100     next year
110     average1 ← total1/365
120     average2 ← total2/365
130     print average1, average2
140  next x
150  print highest, lowest
```

7.3.9
```
10   total ← 0: highest ← 0
20   for x ← 1 to 8000
30      input time
40      speed ← 30/time
50      print speed
60      if speed > 100 then print 'you have exceeded
        speed'
70      if speed > 100 then total ← total + 1
80      if speed > highest then highest = speed
90   next x
100  percent ← total/80
110  print total, percent, highest
```

7.3.10
```
10   input no_players, no_hours
20   cost ← no_players * no_hours * 5
30   if no_players >=3 then discount1 ← cost * 0.25
40   if no_hours > 3 then discount2 ← cost * 0.1
50   cost ← cost – discount1 – discount2
60   print cost
```
Extension hint:
Assume that a file contains all members, so the algorithm will need player to input name and then check if it's on the file. Also input the PIN as four separate digits and

check each digit in turn. If the name and PIN match, the formula in line 20 changes to no_players * no_hours * 4.

Chapter 8

8.4.1

A	B	X
0	0	1
0	1	0
1	0	0
1	1	1

8.4.2

A	B	X
0	0	0
0	1	0
1	0	1
1	1	1

8.4.3

A	B	C	X
0	0	0	0
0	0	1	0
0	1	0	1
0	1	1	0
1	0	0	1
1	0	1	0
1	1	0	1
1	1	1	0

8.4.4

A	B	C	X
0	0	0	0
0	0	1	0
0	1	0	0
0	1	1	1
1	0	0	0
1	0	1	1
1	1	0	0
1	1	1	1

8.4.5

A	B	C	X
0	0	0	0
0	0	1	1
0	1	0	1
0	1	1	0
1	0	0	1
1	0	1	0
1	1	0	0
1	1	1	0

8.4.6

A	B	C	X
0	0	0	0
0	0	1	0
0	1	0	0
0	1	1	0
1	0	0	0
1	0	1	0
1	1	0	0
1	1	1	1

8.4.7 Logic statement:

X = 1 if [R is 1 **AND** S is 1] **OR** [R is **NOT** 1 **AND** (S is 1 **AND** T is 1)]

Logic circuit:

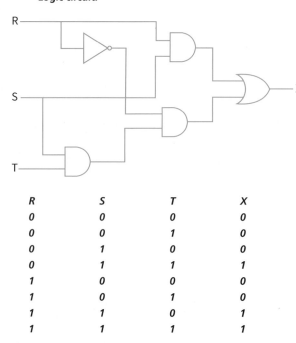

R	S	T	X
0	0	0	0
0	0	1	0
0	1	0	0
0	1	1	1
1	0	0	0
1	0	1	0
1	1	0	1
1	1	1	1

8.4.8 Logic statement:

D = 1 if [A is **NOT** 1] **OR** [A is 1 **AND** (B is **NOT** 1 **AND** C is **NOT** 1)]

Logic circuit:

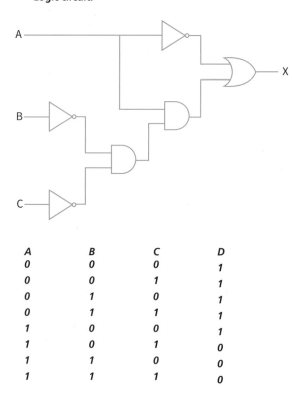

A	B	C	D
0	0	0	1
0	0	1	1
0	1	0	1
0	1	1	1
1	0	0	1
1	0	1	0
1	1	0	0
1	1	1	0

8.4.9 Logic statement:

W = 1 if [C is **NOT** 1] **OR** [T is **NOT** 1 **AND** X = 1] **OR** [C is 1 **AND** T is **NOT** 1]

Logic circuit:

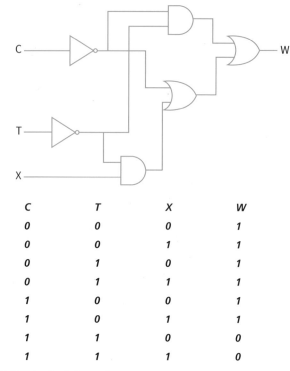

C	T	X	W
0	0	0	1
0	0	1	1
0	1	0	1
0	1	1	1
1	0	0	1
1	0	1	1
1	1	0	0
1	1	1	0

8.4.10 Logic statement:

S = 1 if [T is 1 **AND** W is **NOT** 1] **OR** [T is **NOT** 1 **AND** (P is 1 **OR** W is **NOT** 1)]

Logic circuit:

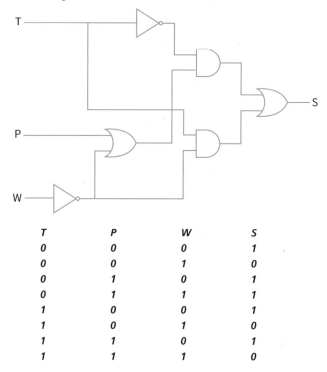

T	P	W	S
0	0	0	1
0	0	1	0
0	1	0	1
0	1	1	1
1	0	0	1
1	0	1	0
1	1	0	1
1	1	1	0

Chapter 9

9.3.1(a)   Free software is where users have the freedom to run, copy, change and adapt available software. The main concept here is one of liberty and not price, since free software guarantees the freedom and rights to study and modify software by having access to the source code itself. Basically, the user controls the program and what it does. There is no need to pay or ask permission to do any of the above since the software has no copyright restrictions. Free software can be commercial or non-commercial in nature. But the original software or modified versions of it must not contain coding from software which doesn't fall into this category since the perpetrator would then fall foul of copyright laws!

Freeware refers to software that anyone can download for free from the Internet and then use without having to pay any fees. The usual copyright laws apply to freeware and the user license is an important part of this. Unlike free software, it is not possible to modify freeware or view the source code.

(b)   Intellectual property rights (for example, is it wrong to copy software without permission?).

Copyright is an important issue with both software types. Since the Internet is fast becoming one of the main areas where copyright issues are becoming a major problem, users need to be careful when downloading this type of software package. Many users of the Internet believe that freedom of information also means that posting or copying any information is exempt from copyright.

(c)   All the features of the full version of the software are not made available and the user has to buy the full version if they intend to use the software in the future. Usually the copyright holder needs to be contacted before copies of the software can be distributed to other people.

9.3.2

Free software: users have the freedom to run, copy, change or adapt this software. The originators of this type of software stress this is based on **liberty** and **not price**. This means that a user is guaranteed the freedom to study and modify the software source code in any way to suit their requirements.

Essentially a user is allowed to do the following:

– run the software for any legal purpose they wish

– study the software source code and modify it where necessary to meet their needs

– the software (in either original or modified form) can be passed on to friends, family or colleagues.

A user of the software doesn't need to seek permission to do any of the above actions since it isn't protected by any copyright restrictions. However, it is important to realise that there are certain rules that need to be obeyed:

– the user cannot add source code from another piece of software unless this is also described as free software

– the user cannot produce software which copies existing software subject to copyright laws

– the user cannot adapt the software in such a way that it infringes copyright laws protecting other software

– the user may not use the source code to produce software which is deemed offensive by third parties.

Freeware: this is software a user can download from the Internet free of charge. Once it has been downloaded, there are no fees associated with using the software. Unlike free software, freeware is subject to copyright laws and users are often requested to tick a box to say they understand and agree to the terms and conditions governing the software. This basically means that a user is not allowed to study or modify the source code in any way.

Shareware: in this case, users are allowed to try out some software free of charge for a trial period. At the end of the trial period, the author of the software will request that user pay a fee if user likes it. Once the fee is paid, a user is registered with the originator of the software and free updates and help are then provided. Very often, the trial version of the software is missing some of the features found in the full version, and these don't become available until the fee is paid. Obviously, this type of software is fully protected by copyright laws and a user must make sure they don't use the source code in any of their own software. Permission needs to be obtained before this software is copied and given to friends, family or colleagues.

Chapter 10

10.6.1 **Data logging**

– This technique involves automatic data collection using sensors.

– Applications include scientific experiments, monitoring the environment.

Barcode readers

– This technique involves reading barcode using laser readers or other types of reader.

– Applications include automatic stock control, automatic ovens, etc.

Rfid

– This method involves minute electronic devices (containing microchip and antenna) and can work from distances of ~5 metres.

- Applications involve tracking of livestock and vehicles, tracking athletes in a race (timing of their event).

Biometrics
- These involve use of unique characteristics of humans, for example, fingerprint scans, retina scans, palm prints, face identification.
- Applications include security systems at airports, entry gates to buildings, security information on passports, etc.

Magnetic stripes
- Magnetic information is stored on a stripe and is automatically read by swiping the stripe through a reader.
- Applications include credit/debit cards, key cards in hotels, etc.

OCR
- This technique involves reading data from hard copy (paper) and converting it automatically to an electronic form.
- Example: this is used to automatically scan documents to check signatures against those stored in memory.

Voice recognition
- These systems recognise the spoken word (voice) patterns and compare them to voice patterns stored in memory.
- These can be used in security systems, can allow disabled people (e.g. blind) to communicate with a computer, etc.

Smart cards
- These contain embedded microchips and receive power from card readers; the chip contains personal data, bank details, etc.
- Applications include credit/debit cards, security cards, loyalty cards, passports (containing biometric data), etc.

OMR
- These systems can read pencil/pen marks on a piece of paper in a pre-defined position, for example, •—•.
- These can be used to automatically read responses in a questionnaire or answers on a multi choice exam paper, etc.

10.6.2 Title – character/type check (must be letters only)
Gender – consistency check (must mate up with *title* field)
Date of birth – format check (should be dd/mm/yyyy)
Pay number – length check (must be exactly 9 digits long)
Telephone number – presence check (this field must be filled in)
Pay per month – range check OR limit check (salary must not exceed $20 000 – but can be any positive value less than that).

10.6.3 (a) 10 9 8 7 6 5 4 3 2 1
   0 –4 5 4 –3 0 0 6 2 –X
(10x0) + (9x4) + (8x5) + (7x4) + (6x3) + (5x0) + (4x0) + (3x6) + (2x2) + (1x10)
= 0 + 36 + 40 + 28 + 18 + 0 + 0 + 18 + 4 + 10
= 154

154 gives NO remainder when divided by 11 hence the check digit is *correct*.

10 9 8 7   6 5 4 3 2   1
   0 –2 1 2 –9 1 1 3 4 –X
(10x0) + (9x2) + (8x1) + (7x2) + (6x9) + (5x1) + (4x1) + (3x3) + (2x4) + (1x10)
= 0 + 18 + 8 + 14 + 54 + 5 + 4 + 9 + 8 + 10
= 130

130 gives a remainder when divided by 11 hence the check digit is *incorrect.*

(b) 10 9 8 7   6 5 4 3 2 1
      0 –5 5 5 –2 1 5 3 3 –?
(10x0) + (9x5) + (8x5) + (7x5) + (6x2) + (5x1) + (4x5) + (3x3) + (2x3)
= 0 + 45 + 40 + 35 + 12 + 5 + 20 + 9 + 6
= 172

This requires the addition of the value **4** to give a number which has NO remainder when divided by 11 hence the check digit is **4.**

10 9 8 7   6 5 4 3 2 1
   0 –1 2 1 –9 0 0 2 1 –?
(10x0) + (9x1) + (8x2) + (7x1) + (6x9) + (5x0) + (4x0) + (3x2) + (2x1)
= 0 + 9 + 16 + 7 + 54 + 0 + 0 + 6 + 2
= 94

This requires the addition of the value **5** to give a number which has NO remainder when divided by 11; hence the check digit is **5.**

(c) Check digits can essentially identify three types of error:
- if 2 digits have been inverted:
  e.g. 23496 instead of 23946
- if an incorrect digit has been input:
  e.g. 23996 instead of 23946
- if a digit has been omitted or an extra digit added:
  e.g. 2396 or 239966 instead of 23946.

10.6.4 (a) Double entry: here data (e.g. from a paper document) is entered *twice* (by two different people) and the computer checks that they match up; an error message is output if there are any discrepancies.

Visual check: as the name suggests, this is a manual system; the original data is compared to data typed in by manually reading it and checking against the original document.

(b) Unlike validation, verification does not check to see if data makes any sense or is within acceptable boundaries – it only checks to see that data entered is identical to data on the original document.

10.6.5 (a) B (hex) =

1	1	1	1

E6 (hex) =

1	1	1	0		0	1	1	0

(b) Hex number is: B 6 F

10.6.6 **(a)** – door sensor and infra red sensor detected intruder in zone 7

– window sensor detected intruder in zone 12

(b)

1	0	0	1	1	1	1	1

10.6.7 **(a)**

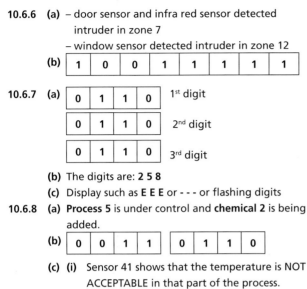

| 0 | 1 | 1 | 0 | 1st digit |

| 0 | 1 | 1 | 0 | 2nd digit |

| 0 | 1 | 1 | 0 | 3rd digit |

(b) The digits are: **2 5 8**

(c) Display such as **E E E** or **- - -** or flashing digits

10.6.8 **(a)** **Process 5** is under control and **chemical 2** is being added.

(b)

0	0	1	1	0	1	1	0

(c) **(i)** Sensor 41 shows that the temperature is NOT ACCEPTABLE in that part of the process.

(ii)

0	0	1	1	0	0	1	1

(iii) hex = B 2

10.6.9 **(a)** 2831

(b) B B 8 (hex)

(c) Any description of error checking (debugging), use in HTML codes, MAC addresses or use in assembly/machine code.

10.6.10 **(a)** Even parity is system which uses an even number of 1-bits to carry out error trapping following transmission of data. It uses a parity bit which is set to 0 if the number already contains an even number of 1s; or it is set to 1 if the number contains an odd number of 1s.

(b) Parity check may not detect an error if more than one bit has been changed and the parity of the received number is correct.

(c) **(i)** the bit in position column 2, row 7 is in error (value = 1)

(ii) column 2 shows odd parity (five 1s) and row 7 also shows odd parity (five 1s); where column 2 and row 7 intersect indicates the bit which has been corrupted.

(d) Any description of checksums, ARQ or other method from elsewhere in textbook.

Chapter 11

11.5.1 **(i)** The processor should consume as little power as possible thereby prolonging internal battery life;

The processor should run as cool as possible minimising the problems associated with heat dissipation;

No fans needed to cool the processor thus reducing the load on the internal battery;

Lightweight; this makes the laptop/notebook completely portable.

(ii) **Advantages:**

They are portable;

Do not require a supply of electricity (battery power).

Disadvantages:

More expensive than equivalent desktop computer;

Easier to steal;

Lower specification than desktop (i.e. memory size, processor power);

Greater security risk (if stolen and sensitive data is stored on the hard drive).

11.5.2 **(a)** **Washing machine:**

Control of water temperature;

Time for each part of the wash cycle;

Control the wash cycle (add water, rinse, etc.);

Loading (i.e. weight of clothes in drum).

Digital camera:

Shutter speed;

Lens focussing (sharpness of image);

Control of flash (automatically set off flash, etc.);

Aperture (amount of light entering camera).

Television set:

Automatic tuning into television stations;

Allow digital signals to be decoded;

Constantly monitor signals – so better sound and picture quality;

Allows interface with many devices (e.g. games machines);

Built in diagnostics in case of malfunction;

Modular design (easier maintenance);

Microprocessors allow stereo sound, 3D broadcast.

11.5.3 **(a)** **Dot matrix printer**

Advantages:

– They work with continuous (fan folded) stationery which means they can do very large print jobs without any human interaction.

– They work with multi-part stationery which means 'carbon copies' can be made immediately.

– Relatively inexpensive to run and maintain.

– Can work in damp and dirty atmospheres (e.g. on a factory floor) – an environment which would cause problems for the other two printers.

– Able to print raised characters (i.e. Braille to allow blind or partially-sighted people to read the outputs).

Disadvantages:

– They are relatively expensive to purchase in the first place.

– They tend to be very noisy in operation.

– Printing is slow and usually of a very poor quality compared to laser and inkjet.

– Although they do work in colour (usually a 4-colour ribbon), the results are very limited – they certainly couldn't be used to print out a photo.

Inkjet printer

Advantages:

- they are very cheap to purchase in the first place
- they produce high quality output; used to produce photographs
  relatively quiet in operation

Disadvantages:

- Ink cartridges don't last very long – this makes the printers unsuitable for any long print runs (e.g. printing a colour magazine).
- Printing can 'smudge' if touched too early or the wrong paper type is used.
- Relatively expensive to run (mainly due to the cost of ink cartridges).

Laser printers

Advantages:

- Very low noise levels.
- Fast output and well suited to high volume printing.
- Toner cartridges last a long time (can be cost effective when compared to inkjet printers).
- Print quality is extremely good.

Disadvantages:

- Maintenance and running costs can be expensive (e.g. colour toner cartridges and replacement of diffuser packs are expensive).
- They produce ozone and volatile organic matter which can be harmful to some people when the printer is used in an office environment.

The company would need to use a dot matrix on the factory floor due to potentially damp or dusty atmosphere. A laser printer would be best suited to the office where it's near silent printing and ability to cope with high volumes of printouts makes it ideal.

(b) Administration work – keyboards, mouse
Design and research – light pen, trackerball, spaceball
Video conferencing – webcams, microphone
Security – various sensors, keypad for codes

(c) Touch screen/head wand:

- These devices are used for people who cannot use a keyboard to input information into a computer; menu options or letters appear on a touch screen which just need to be touched by a device such as **head wand.**

Microphones:

- Blind or partially-sighted people can use microphones to input data into a computer; their voice is converted into an electronic form using software called **voice recognition** and, once understood by the computer, can be manipulated like any other data.

Loud speakers:

- **Voice synthesis software** is used to output sound/voices to users who are disabled (e.g. blind) or

have difficulty reading/understanding text; loud speakers are used to output the sounds/voice.

Trackerball:

- These devices are easier to use than a mouse if people have problems using their hands and arms or if they have coordination problems.

Braille printer:

- These use old technology dot matrix printers which can produce output in the form of raised dots (i.e. Braille characters) which can be read by blind or partially-sighted people.

Large/concept keyboard:

- These help people who have difficulty using normal keyboards (due to difficulty using hands/arms or coordination problems).

11.5.4 (a) Characteristics of RAM

- They are **volatile** memories (i.e. the contents are lost on switching off the computer).
- They store the file/data temporarily that the user is working on.
- These memories can be written to and read from and the contents can be changed by the user.

Characteristics of ROM

- They are **non-volatile** permanent memories (which means the contents are not lost when the power is turned off).
- The contents can be read only (they cannot be modified).
- The ROM often holds the instructions for starting up the computer (often referred to as the **BIOS (basic input/output system)**).

(b) Multimedia files – DVD/CD (large memory capacity)
Music files – MP3 (uses music format)
Word processor – CD/memory stick (number of
doc   small files)
Back up files – portable hard drive (files/software may be large), memory stick (very portable media)
Security camera – DVD-RAM (record and playback at same time).

11.5.5 (a) 4 Mbyte

(b) More robust, much larger memory capacity

11.5.6 (a) Touch screens; Mouse/trackerball; Concept keyboards; Light pens

(b) – The system can be linked into websites (very useful option at airports, bus or railway stations where it is possible to have 'live' arrivals and departures boards).

- Because it is easier/faster to update (and ALL kiosks/desks will display the same information), the information is usually more up to date and accurate.
- There are no language problems (language options can be given on screen and the customer

selects the most appropriate one); man-operated desks would have a limited language capability.

- Customers don't have to wait in queues.
- The kiosks/desks are open 24/7 since they are un-manned.

(c)
- Lower costs (fewer staff required);
- Can advertise special offers;
- Can deal with customers faster (improves their reputation).

(d) Local attractions, local time, location of platforms, facilities at station

11.5.7 (a) Such monitors consist of a front layer of LCD (liquid crystal diode/display) that makes up the image from a number of pixels. This LCD layer is then back-lit using LEDs which give it better brightness and contrast. LEDs have several advantages over the older CCFC (cold cathode fluorescent lamp) technology used to back-lit LCD monitors in the past:

- They reach their maximum brightness almost immediately (no need to 'warm up')
- They give a 'whiter' tint sharpening the image and making it look more 'vivid'; CCFCs gave a yellowish tint
- They produce a brighter light than CCFCs allowing the picture to be much brighter in appearance
- The monitors are now much thinner due to the use of LEDs
- Since LEDs last almost indefinitely, this technology is much more reliable and consistent
- Since LEDs consume very little power, LCDs back-lit with this technology are very energy efficient

(b) (i) Thermal bubble and piezoelectric

(ii) Thermal uses heat to generate a bubble which expands and ejects ink onto the paper; piezoelectric uses a vibrating crystal which forces ink out of a nozzle onto the paper.

(c) (i) Inkjet printers use liquid ink which is ejected onto paper either by heating to create bubbles of ink or by vibrating crystals; laserjet uses dry ink (known as toner) which forms letters and images on paper by electrostatic attraction – this ink is fixed to the paper by heating it until it melts using a fuser.

(ii) Ozone gas is produced because of the use of lasers and electrostatic charges and also toner particles can enter the air which are breathed in by office workers.

(d) The printer receives the data and stores it in a printer buffer (temporary memory); this allows the computer to send data to the printer quickly and, while the printing process is being carried out, the computer can get on with other tasks (printing is a relatively slow process).

11.5.8 (a) (i) 5 min 20 seconds = 320 seconds

216 000 x 320 = 65 120 000 byte = 62.10 Mbyte

(assumes 1 Mbyte = 1 048 576 bytes)

(ii) 12 files would occupy 12 x 62.10 = 683.1 Mbyte

(b) 56 megabits/second = 7 Mbyte/second

683.1/7 = 97.6 seconds to download all 12 files

(c) 68.3 Mbyte (approx)

11.5.9 (a) Passport scanners are now used at airports to scan data from passports. It uses OCR technology to provide high quality digital images of the scanned document in a format that can be understood by a computer. The data is usually stored in a database which allows easy searching and manipulation of the data.

The system will automatically:

- Identify a scanned document
- Locate the required text and images
- Carry out any required error detection
- Store the text in an ASCII file format.

(b) (i) Barcode technology is used in most supermarkets around the world at the checkouts where each barcode is scanned by a barcode reader/scanner. The barcode is looked up in a database (the barcode number is usually the key field for searching purposes) and once the required item is found, details such as price and description are sent back to the checkout (or point of sale (POS) terminal). The item is also 'flagged' as being sold and the new quantity in stock written back to the appropriate record in the database. This quantity of stock is compared to the minimum order/stock level and if it is equal to this value, or less, then an automatic re-order for new stock is generated by the computer.

(ii) Keyboard/keypad, touch screen, credit/debit card reader, loudspeaker/beeper

uses:

- key in barcode number if scanner fails to read barcode/key in number of same items
- select items (such as fruit or bread) from a screen since fresh fruit may not have a barcode
- magnetic stripe/chip and PIN device to read data from customer's card to enable payment to be made
- produce sound to confirm barcode read correctly OR to indicate an error if barcode failed to read.

11.5.10 (a) *Lossless file compression* is based on the idea that files can be broken down into files of 'similar size' for transmission or storage, and then put back together again at the receiving end so it can be used again.

Lossy file compression works differently to lossless file compression. Lossy compression algorithms eliminate unnecessary bits of information (refer to jpeg system described earlier, for example). It becomes impossible to get back to the original file once this lossy compression algorithm has been applied and the new file stored.

(b) *Jpeg* is an image encoding system that compresses photographs and other images. It is a lossy format (see later) and makes use of certain properties of human vision to eliminate certain unnecessary information.

It is a very complex process which goes way beyond the scope of this book. Putting it in simple terms, it relies on the human eye being unable to distinguish colours of similar brightness or similar hues. A typical RGB (red, green, blue) bit map image is converted to a YCbCr image (where Y = brightness of the pixel, Cb/Cr = chroma, which are the blue and red differences, respectively); these images are considerably smaller in size than the original.

(c) faster to upload/download files when sending over the Internet.

(d)

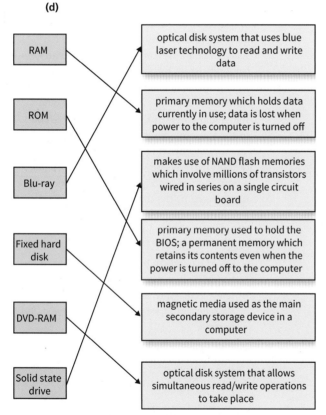

Chapter 12

12.9.1 (a) – Provides a user interface
- Multitasking
- Batch processing (JCL)
- Multiprogramming
- Error reporting/handling
- Loading/running software

- Maintain user accounts
- Utilities
- Processor management
- Memory management
- Spooling
- Handling interrupts
- Maintain security
- Input/output control.

(b) Many household devices contain microprocessors. However, many of these devices do not require an operating system (e.g. dish washer and refrigerator). The microprocessor has just one set of tasks to perform; the system expects simple inputs (e.g. a keypad on the front of the dish washer) and they have simple, never-changing hardware functions to control. Thus, an operating system is not necessary, leading to lower costs for both development and manufacturing stages.

12.9.2 *Real time process control* is very different to real time transaction processing. With real time process control, sensors and feedback loops are used (essentially, the output can influence the next input to the system). This type of processing doesn't involve updating databases or customer accounts, for example.

12.9.3 (a) Address, data and control

(b) Memory, processor, control unit and input/output interface

12.9.4 (a) Memory address register
Memory data register

(b) (i) 1001 1000

(ii) Memory location 111001 would now contain value 1011 1010

(c) MBR – memory buffer register
CIR – current instruction register
PC – program counter

12.9.5

Description of stage	Order of carrying out each stage
Address contained in PC is copied to MAR via address bus	2
Address part of instruction is placed in MAR	6
Entire instruction is then copied from MBR and placed in CIR	4
Instruction is finally decoded and then executed	7
Instruction is then copied from memory location contained in MAR and is placed in MBR	3
PC contains the address of the next instruction to be fetched	1
Value in the PC is then incremented so that it points to the next instruction to be fetched	5

12.9.6 **(a)** – Transmission of several bits along a number of wires

– Data can travel in one direction only

(b) – Data transmitted one bit at a time over a single wire

– Data can flow in both directions but not in both directions at the same time

12.9.7 **(a) Asynchronous**

With *asynchronous* transmission, signals are sent in a previously agreed pattern of bits. The bits being sent are grouped together and consist of actual data and *control bits*. In other words, a *start bit* is sent at the beginning of the group of data and a *stop bit* is sent at the end of the group of data. This therefore informs the receiver where the transmitted group of bits starts and where it ends. Otherwise it would be impossible to distinguish when each group of bits is being received.

Synchronous

Synchronous transmission is a data transfer method where a continuous stream of data is also accompanied by timing signals (generated by the internal electronic clock) to ensure sender and receiver are in step (i.e. synchronised with each other). With this method, the receiver counts the bits sent and then reassembles the bytes. It is essential that timing is maintained as there are no start and stop bits and no gaps (as in asynchronous transmission). Accuracy is dependent on the receiver keeping an accurate count of the bits as they come in.

(b) (i)

Hardware devices are automatically detected and can be configured when first attached (loads up device driver)
USB connectors are shaped so that it is not possible to install devices incorrectly
The USB standard is an 'open standard' and has considerable industry support
USB connectivity supports many different data transmission speeds and data transfer types
The latest USB 2.0 standard is backward compatible with the older USB 1.1 standard

(ii)

Cable length is limited to 5 metres
Transmission speed is limited to 480 megabits/second (Mbps)
USB support may not be available for very long when using older devices or earlier operating systems

Chapter 13

Sample paper 1

The following answers are to be used as guidelines when using these papers as revision exercises. They should at least provoke discussion since alternative answers are possible in many of the questions.

Readers are advised to refer to the text in chapters 1 to 12 and also refer to other Computer Science textbooks when evaluating performance on these sample papers.

1
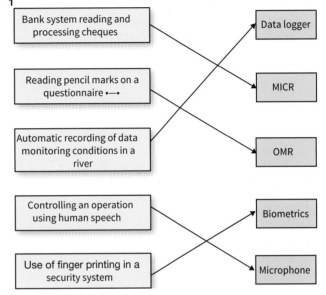

2 **(a)** Any **four** from:
- pH sensor sends signals to the computer
- Signal converted into digital by ADC
- Computer compares pH value with stored value
- If pH too low, then computer sends signal
- (converted into analogue by DAC)
- Actuator opens valve to admit acid
- Actuator starts motor to turn stirrer
- Monitoring continues until process finished.

(b) Any **two** from:
- Instantaneous reaction/response if a fault occurs
- No need to have people present to constantly monitor process
- If reaction is dangerous, this is a safer method
- Can automatically collect data and store for later analysis
- Does not get tired or make errors.

(c) monitoring

any **one** from:
- Sensor values are compared to stored values
- If out of range, computer sends signal to sound alarm (etc.).

control

any **one** from:
- Sensor values are compared to stored values
- If out of range, computer sends signal to later the process to bring values into line
- Output affects the input.

3 Phishing   – do not open emails if sender is unknown to you

   Hacking   – use of passwords

   – use of firewalls

   Viruses   – anti-virus software

   – don't download from unknown websites

   War driving– secure Internet connections using passwords

   Fraud   – use of data encryption

4 Laserjet printer   – printing colour brochures

   – high speed, high quality, colour printing possible

   dot matrix printer – printing invoices, quality control sheets in a factory

   – no need for high quality, can produce 'carbon copies', can work in damp and dusty atmospheres

   3D printer   – computer-aided design

   – can produce solid working models relatively cheaply.

5

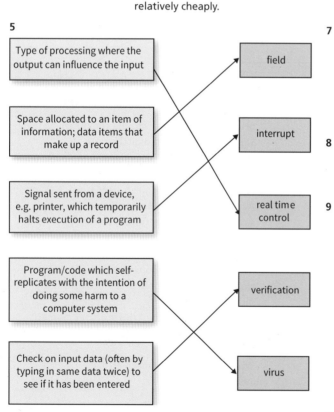

6 **(a) working out** (1 mark per square bracket):

A = 1 if [W = 1 **OR** D = 1 **AND** F = **NOT** 1] **OR**

[W = **NOT** 1 **AND** D = **NOT** 1 **AND** F =1]

logic circuit:

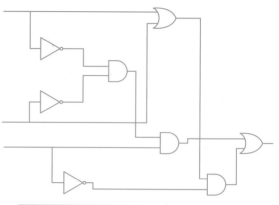

(b)

W	D	F	A
0	0	0	0
0	0	1	1
0	1	0	1
0	1	1	0
1	0	0	1
1	0	1	0
1	1	0	1
1	1	1	0

7 (a) 0 0 1 0

0 1 1 1

0 0 1 1

(b) 1 4 9

(c) 9 9 9

(d) – No need to interpret an instrument

– Easier to read

8 (a) Binary = 1 1 0 0 1 0 1 0

Hex = B A

(b) (i) 1 0 0 1 0 1 1 1

(ii) A 7

9 (a) Even number of 1s in the binary number

if an even number of 1s already, 0 is placed in parity bit position

if an odd number of 1s, a 1 is placed in parity bit position

(b) (i) Column 7

Row 3

(ii) Byte 3 has an odd number of 1s/odd parity

column 7 contains a number with odd number of 1s/odd parity

Where column 7 and row 3 meet gives incorrect bit/bit in position (3,7) should be a 0 and not a 1.

Sample paper 2

The following answers are to be used as guidelines when using these papers as revision exercises. They should at least provoke discussion since alternative answers are possible in many of the questions. Readers are advised to refer to the text in chapters 1 to 12 and also refer to other Computer Science text books when evaluating performance on these sample papers.

1   (a) StudentNames[1..20]
           StudentTimes[1..20]

     (b)
         – Outside loops zeroing total, fastest and slowest
         – Two loops one for task 1
         – And one for task 2
         – In task 1 loop input name and times
         – Check for time > 300
         – Store in appropriate position in arrays
         – Put marker in time array if disqualified, for example, –1
         – In task 2 loop adding to the students' total time
         – Checking for fastest
         – Replacing fastest when necessary
         – Checking for slowest
         – Replacing slowest when necessary
         – Not including disqualified students in total time or slowest
         – Outside loop calculating class average time
         – Printing class average time

Sample algorithm:
```
Total ← 0: Fastest ← 300: Slowest ← 0
FOR Count ← 1 TO 20
        INPUT Name
        StudentNames[Count] ← Name
        INPUT Time
        If Time <= 300 THEN StudentTimes[Count] ← Time
                        ELSE StudentTimes[Count] ← –1
NEXT Count
ValidTimes ← 0
FOR Count ← 1 TO 20
        IF StudentTimes[Count] < Fastest AND
        StudentTimes[Count] <> –1
        THEN Fastest ← StudentTimes[Count]
        IF StudentTimes[Count] > Slowest THEN Slowest ←
        StudentTimes[Count]
        IF StudentTimes[Count] <> –1
        THEN
        Total ← Total + StudentTimes[Count]
        ValidTimes ← ValidTimes + 1
NEXT Count
Average ← Total/ValidTimes
PRINT Average
```

     (c) *Many correct answers, these are examples only*
          Set 1: 10, 10, 10, 10, 10, 10, 10, 10, 10, 10, 10, 10, 10, 10, 10, 10, 10, 10, 10, 10
          Reason: valid data to check the result of calculating the average time
          Set 2: 350, 301, 300, 300, 300, 300, 300, 300, 300, 300, 300, 300, 300, 300, 300, 300, 300, 300, 300, 300, 300, 300,

Reason: data to check that times on the boundary of the range check are accepted and that slower times are dealt with appropriately

     (d) (i) *Many correct answers, this is an example only*
          – Copy array StudentTimes[1..20] to TempTimes[1..20]
          – Set Array FastestTime[1..3] to 300 and Array BestName[1..3] to blanks
          – Use an outer loop for the three fastest times
          – Loop 20 times to check each student's time in turn
          – Using TempTimes[count] check student's time against FastestTime[i]
          – If student's time < FastestTime[i] then …
          – … Replace value in FastestTime[i] by student's time and store student's name in BestName[i] keep a copy of the counter
          – In outer loop replace TempTimes[counter] with a large number, for example, 300
          – Outside outer loop output FastestTime[1..3] and array BestName[1..3]

Sample algorithm:
```
FOR i ← 1 TO 20
        TempTimes[i] ← StudentTimes[i]
NEXT i
FOR i ← 1 TO 3
        FastestTime [i] ← 0
        BestName[i] ← ""
NEXT i
FOR i ← 1 TO 3
        FOR Count ← 1 TO 20
                IF StudentTimes[Count] < FastestTime[i]
                THEN
                        FastestTime[i] ← TempTimes[Count]
                        BestName[i] ← StudentNames[Count]
                        CopyCount ← Count
                ENDIF
        NEXT Count
        TempTimes[CopyCount] ← 400
NEXT i
FOR i ← 1 TO 3
        PRINT FastestTime[i], BestName[i]
NEXT i
```
If algorithm or program code only then max 3 marks

          (ii) comment on which students' names could be missing

2   (a) name of person   – character check
          today's date   – format check
                            – length check
          price of annual   – range check
                            – character check
          Year of annual   – range check
                            – format check
                            – length check
                            – character check

     (b) limited number of options possible

     (c) Any **two** from:

– <u>Computer</u> check on input data ....
  – ... check to see if data satisfies certain criteria/is reasonable
  – ... data is within acceptable boundaries
(d) Any **three** from:
  – Extra digit added to a number
  – It is calculated from the other digits based on their position within the number
  – At the receiving end, another computer re-calculates the check digit
  – ... and compares its value to that with the sent data
  – Many systems use the modulo-11 method

3

X	mark	D	M	P	F	OUTPUT
		0	0	0	0	
1	78	1				distinction
2	51		1			merit
3	23				1	fail
4	60		2			merit
5	70	2				distinction
6	50			1		pass
7	4				2	fail
8	80	3				distinction
9	44			2		pass
10	39			3		pass
11						3, 2, 3, 2

4 **(a)** **1** total not set to zero insert *total* = 0 before **2** **repeat**
 2 4 test wrong should read **if** x > 0...
 3 6 **print** *total* should be outside loop
 (b) – Compiler Produces Object Code/Interpreter Doesn't Produce Object Code
  – Compiler Translates Whole Program In One Go/Interpreter Translates And Executes Line At A Time
  – Compiler Produces List Of All Errors/Interpreter Produces Error Message Each Time An Error Encountered
  – Compiler Produces 'Stand Alone Code'/Interpreter Doesn't Produce 'Stand Alone Code'
  – Compilation Process Is Slow But Resultant Code Runs Very quickly/interpreted code runs slowly

16 **Marking points:**
 • Initialisation
 • Loop
 • Total height calculation
 • Count number of floors > 50
 • Find highest
 • Calculate average height
 • Output OUTSIDE the loop
 • Input INSIDE the loop

sample program:
  total ≠ 0: highest ≠ 0: no_floors ≠ 0
  for c ≠ 1 **to** 200
   input height, floors
   total ≠ total + height
      if floors > 50 **then** no_floors ≠ no_floors + 1
      if height > highest **then** highest ≠ height
  next c
  average_height ≠ total/200
  print average_height, no_floors, highest

6
pendown	FORWARD 20
LEFT 90	PENDOWN
forward 20	FORWARD 40/REPEAT
RIGHT 90/REPEAT	RIGHT 90/FORWARD 40
FORWARD 20/RIGHT 90	FORWARD 40/RIGHT 90
RIGHT 90/FORWARD 20	RIGHT 90/ENDREPEAT
- - - - - - - - - - - - - - - -	- - - - - - - - - - - - - - - -
LEFT 90/REPEAT	FORWARD 20/REPEAT
FORWARD 20/LEFT 90	LEFT 90/FORWARD 20
LEFT 90/FORWARD 20	FORWARD 20/LEFT 90
FORWARD 20/ENDREPEAT	LEFT 90/ENDREPEAT
- - - - - - - - - - - - - - - -	- - - - - - - - - - - - - - - -
RIGHT 90/REPEAT	FORWARD 20/REPEAT
FORWARD 40/RIGHT 90	RIGHT 90/FORWARD 20
RIGHT 90/FORWARD 40	FORWARD 20/RIGHT 90
FORWARD 40/ENDREPEAT	RIGHT 90/ENDREPEAT
PENUP	FORWARD 20
- - - - - - - - - - - - - - - -	- - - - - - - - - - - - - - - -

15 **Marking points:**
 • Initialisation
 • Inputs
 • Check if finish > start or vice versa
 • Calculate fare between start end finish
 • Calculate cost of tickets
 • Calculate discount if > 3 passengers
 • Loop to control input of money
 • Calculate money added to machine
 • Loop to print out required number of tickets
 • Output tickets

Sample program:
  total ≠ 0: reduction ≠ 0
  input passengers
  input start, finish
   if finish > start **then** fare ≠ finish – start
      else if start > finish **then** fare ≠ start – finish
      cost ≠ fare * 20 * passengers
      if passengers > 3 **then** cost ≠ cost * 0.9
  repeat
      input money
      total ≠ total + money
  until total = cost
  for x ≠ 1 **to** passengers
      print ticket
  next x

Index

Acknowledgements

Thanks to the following sources for permission to reproduce photographs:

p. 2*t* Denis Rozhnovsky/Shutterstock; p. 2*b*, Maksym Bondarchuk/Shutterstock; p. 3*l*, hadescom/ shutterstock; p. 3*r* S1001/Shutterstock; p. 13 Federico Rostagno/Shutterstock; p. 22*l* Alexey D. Vedernikov/ Shutterstock; p. 22*r* tuanyick/Shutterstock; p. 24*l* Palto/Shutterstock; p. 24*r* Gravvi/Shutterstock; p. 28 Imagery ©2015 Infoterra Ltd & Bluesky, Landsat, map data ©2015 Google; p. 127 Valeri Potapova/ Shutterstock; p. 129 Bayanova Svetlana/Shutterstock; p. 130 Grandpa/Shutterstock; p. 133 Piero Cruciatti/ Alamy; p. 135 nerijus jurevicius/Thinkstock; p. 142-143 Vendor/Shutterstock

page position *t* = top, *b* = bottom, *l* = left, *r* = right